QURAN FOR CHILDREN

ABDUL RAUF

EDITED AND REVISED BY

LALEH BAKHTIAR

Library of Islam

Book designer

Liaquat Ali

Library of Congress Cataloging in Publication Data

Rauf, A.
Quran for Children.
1. Islam. 2. Quran. 3. Juvenile Literature.
ISBN: 0-935782-08-7

Published by the Library of Islam
P. O. Box 595
South Elgin IL 60177

Distributed by
KAZI Publications, Inc.
3023 W. Belmont Avenue
Chicago IL 60618
Tel: 312-267-7001; FAX: 312-267-7002

CONTENTS

5 Negative Traits to be Avoided

6 Self-Development

7 Prayers of Peace and Progress

To Prophet Muhammad (ﷺ)
to whom was revealed the Quran,
the inspiration and the guidance
for all children of the world

Dear Kian,

This is for you dear on the 1st Day of Spring, 1999,
Persian New Year 1374.

May this ancient wisdom bring
you happiness.

love, Katy

Preface to the First Edition

Outlined in the pages that follow is an easy-to-understand code of practical guidance for all those who are eager to develop their character and personality after the creative patterns spelled out in the Holy Quran. This small book is designed to serve a useful purpose especially for the following categories of young readers:

* Children residing in English speaking parts of the modern world;
* Children studying in schools where the medium of education is English;
* Children who are desirous of improving their knowledge of Islam and incidentally of Arabic and English languages:
* Children who want to acquire a working familiarity with the Holy Quran.

Quran for Children, however, is not meant for children alone. Parents, teachers, and all adults who may wish to understand the dynamic potentialities of the Holy Quran in shaping children's thought and behavior will also find this eye-opening book a rewarding study and a satisfying experience.

A. R.
1985

Notes to the Instructor

Arabic is a Semetic language and as such differs substantially in grammar and syntax from English. The student may notice differences between the translation and transliteration of the Arabic text when given completely and those given in the word by word version under the Arabic script. While the full translation is meant to convey the idiomatic meaning of the phrase, the word by word rendering focuses on the literal and core meaning of individual words. The student may also note differences in the transliteration when words are treated out of context as discrete items, particularly at the end and in the beginning in the case of words made definite by the article "*al*." A number of words implied or excess in one language or the other, usually prepositions and the definite article "the/*al*," are included in parentheses to give the flavor of the Arabic usage or when necessary in English usage.

The definite article (*al*, the) is used more frequently in Arabic than English. It is used with abstract nouns with a general sense such as poverty, kindness, etc. whereas it is not in English. In addition, the article is used with modifying adjectives. "The red house" would in Arabic be rendered "the house the red."

Many proper names including Islam, Iraq, Jordan, Sudan, etc. take the definite article in Arabic. To further complicate matters, in the case of the so-called "sun letters," the "*l*" of "*al*" is changed in pronunciation (but not in writing) according to the sound of the following consonant. Thus the word for sun (*shams*) when definite is written "*al-shams*" but pronounced "*ash-shams*." In contrast, "*qamar*" (moon), when definite, retains the "*l*" in pronunciation: "*al-qamar*" (the moon). A list of the sun and moon letters can be found in any standard Arabic grammar.

There is yet another complication with the article "*al*." Not only can the "*l*" change, but the vowel "*a*" when it begins a phrase or happens to coincide with an "*a*" inflection of the preceding word. Otherwise, it may be "*il*" or "*ul*," depending upon the preceding vowel. To summarize, the "*a*" of "*al*" may change according to the preceding vowel and the "*l*" may change according to the following consonant.

Other changes, fortunately, not so many as in the case with "*al*" may also occur at the juncture of words in a phrase. "N" is particularly susceptible. While still being written "n," if followed by "b" is pronounced "m." Thus the phrase "*min ba*^{c}*d*" (after) is pronounced "*mim ba*^{c}*d*." "N" may also change to r, l. w, etc. Remember that doubled consonants are always doubled in pronunciation in contrast to English.

It should be noted that the past tense in Arabic is frequently used with a present or even future meaning, especially in conditional sentences, wishes, and in formula phrases that in English usually begin with "May he/she/it..." etc.

May God reward you in this sacred task.

1
Introduction

This small book has been especially prepared for the children of the modern age. It presents a selection of easy-to-understand verses from the Quran. These verses offer new pleasures, new hope and new determination to the reader. Even a cursory reading will help in improving one's everyday life.

The Holy Quran offers practical guidance about all aspects of life. Whether one is living in the East or the West, is a Muslim or a non-Muslim, one has the right to enjoy the beauties of the Quran. This way is the surest way of developing one's personality and character.

This small book follows a clear plan and a constructive purpose. It presents a selection of only those verses of the Quran that have a special relevance to a child's life. Experience has shown that children stand to gain a great deal from such guiding verses.

There are seven chapters in this book. This is the opening chapter. It offers an introduction to the Quran and its relevance to a child's life. The next chapter is a selection of verses about God and our relation to God. The third chapter presents an easy to understand explanation of the fundamentals of Islam in light of some simple Quranic verses. The title of the fourth chapter is, "Fruits of Moral Behavior." It offers a summary of all that is good in life which children must understand and practice for their benefit. The fifth chapter highlights the wrongdoing of such things as lying, aggression, fostering unhealthy thought patterns and joining in with unhealthy company. How does the Quran prepare children for discipline and sound development? A brief answer is available in the sixth chapter. The last chapter offers a selection of some simple Quranic prayers. They are a source of immense joy and self-confidence. Such prayers play a manifold role. They help children face life and its challenges in a cheerful and confident way.

Each one of the above chapters opens with a brief summary of the entire theme under discussion. That is followed by selected verses illustrating the theme further. Both literal and free translations of each verse are given. At the end of each verse, reference has been given to the part, chapter and verse where it is found in the Quran so that those children who intend to pursue the subject further may do so.

Section 1: Interesting Facts About the Quran

The Quran is the Divine Book of Muslims. It is a revealed Book. This means that it is not a product of human endeavor. It is a collection of Messages from God Almighty. It is meant for the guidance of all peoples of the world.

These Divine Messages were revealed to the Messenger (ﷺ) from time to time. His Companions used to record the same in writing so that they could be preserved for humanity. The Messages were initially recorded on dried animal skins, camel bones, mud slabs, stone plates, tree bark, palm leaves, etc. Later on, with the availability of paper and printing facilities, the same were reproduced and preserved in the form in which you find it today.

The Quran is divided into thirty parts. Each part contains a number of chapters devoted to various problems of life. A chapter is called *surah*. It is composed of rhyming lines known as *ayah* or Signs, verses. The total number of the *surahs* is 114. Every *surah* but one opens with the phrase, "In the Name of God, the Merciful, the Compassionate."

The Quran was originally revealed in Arabic. Its translations have been rendered into all major languages of the world. It has proven to be the most wholesome, the most comprehensive and the most practical guide for all sectors of human life. All shades of people in all parts of the world have availed of its immensely useful Message.

Muslims respect the Quran. It is as dear to them as life itself. They recite the verses in their daily prescribed prayers. In addition, they also recite it during the daytime for guidance and spiritual development to grow closer to God. The body and dress of the reader must be pure and the place where one is reading must be clean.

History shows that those individuals and nations which studied the Quran and acted upon it, flourished in all fields of life. They made the lives of others around them equally pleasant and productive. The Quran is now the world's most widely respected Book.

Section 2: How the Quran Was Completed

The Messenger (ﷺ) spent fifty-three years of his life in Makkah and the last ten years in Madinah. Some verses of the Quran were revealed in Makkah while the remaining parts were revealed in Madinah. The entire series of this Divine communication lasted for twenty-three years. It began in 13 BH (basically in Makkah before the migration to Madinah) and ended in 10 AH (after the migration to Madinah). Every year during the month of Ramadan, the Messenger (ﷺ) would tell the scribes what chapter (*surah*) each verse (*ayah*) was a part of and the order of the chapters. These were collected in their original form and saved during the caliphate of Abu Bakr as-Siddiqi, the first rightly-guided caliph. They were put together in a book form for circulation in various parts of the then known world during the time of the third rightly-guided caliph, Uthman ibn Affan. Ever since that day, this Book, the original Arabic of which has not changed, has guided the destiny of humanity.

Section 3: Advantages of Reading the Quran

Life today is filled with risks and danger. Daily events and situations often yield depression, anxiety, tension and insecurity Teachers and parents are worried. They often wonder if, under the present conditions, their children can develop into useful citizens.

Whatever kind of situation you live in, the Quran is there to help you. You will find that it offers solutions to your problems and perplexities. It provides concrete guidance about all that is good, beautiful and pleasant. A study of the Quran will open up the doors of hope, confidence, vitality and achievement. You will feel like growing into a new, energetic and constructive person.

In short, if you are really interested in moving forward in life, this book is going to serve a real purpose for you. Quranic Arabic is the simplest. Try to understand the meaning of these verses with the help of the literal translation given underneath each Arabic word. Try to grasp the idea and purpose in each verse.

If you like a verse, and you are bound to like many, try to memorize its original Arabic text, or, at least the translation. This will enrich your thinking, vitalize your speech and polish your writing. Your attitude and behavior will assume a meaningful direction. It is so easy to remember Quranic verses because of their rhythm and sounds. That is why the Quran is the only revealed Book in the world which so many are able to just naturally memorize. At the moment there are several hundred thousand men and women, as well as a large number of children in various parts of the world who have committed the whole of the Quran to memory without difficulty.

The Quranic verses speak of life. These could be easily used in everyday conversation, debates and writings. Let us suppose that you are thinking, talking, discussing or writing about children and their parents. Such Quranic verses as pertain to the children's role in life and duties of the parents about education and recreation of children could help you a great deal in thinking clearly on the subject. The Quran has much to offer for such vital issues as: the meaning, purpose and utility of goodness, beauty, honesty, justice and hard work in everyday life. It speaks volumes against the evils of irrational differentiation based on color, caste, creed or country. Instead, it advocates the supremacy of piety, equality and good behavior. The Quran offers powerful motivation for purposeful labor, honest dealings and absolute justice in all human activities.

Needless to say that once you start appreciating such ennobling ideas, your power of thinking, speaking and writing will improve. It will assume entirely new dimensions. But you are not to let the effect of these enchanting verses be confined to your thinking and writing alone. These verses possess an astonishing power to transform people's character and conduct. This could happen with you, as well. Just try to put the new idea into practice. You will then discover that your everyday behavior changes. Practice these virtues in your daily life. You will find that you are becoming a better and a still better person from day to day.

So why delay! Why not start understanding these verses right now? Endeavor to practice them in everyday situations. You will then never be overpowered by such troublesome factors as anxiety, frustration, lack of will, temptation to steal, lie or deceive others. There could be no better way of generating joy, energy and confidence in all walks of life at home, in school and in society at large.

Section 4 : Why should we read *Quran for Children*?

One may ask, "Why should a child growing up in the modern world read this book?" As a matter of fact, the purposes and the utility of this book are many. Some of the basic aims and advantages of going through such a guidance are the following:

1. Stimulating interest in the Quran
2. Preparing for a successful life.
3. Promoting familiarity with Arabic.
4. Offering a code of child guidance.
5. Enriching knowledge of non-Muslims.

Stimulating Interest in the Quran

This book offers an easy to understand introduction to the Quran. The style and presentation are appropriate for the mental level of children. The idea is to stimulate child interest in the Quran so that he or she feels like studying, enjoying and practicing it conveniently during various stages of his or her life.

Preparing for a Successful Life

The Quran offers a constructive program for all areas of life. One of the basic objectives of this book is to motivate children to lead an active life in developing their character and personality.

Promoting Familiarity with Arabic

Another useful aim is to familiarize children with the Arabic language. Arabic, as you may know, is the language spoken by millions of people but above this, it is the language that God chose to give the last revelation. The easiest way of understanding Arabic is to study the Quran because its language is the simplest possible Arabic. It is interesting to note that unlike the English language, Arabic is written and read from right to left.

Offering a Code of Child Guidance

Yet another constructive purpose of this book is to help parents and teachers in understanding and handling their children. It provides them with a practical, wholesome and trustworthy code of child guidance based on the Quran.

Enriching Knowledge of Non-Muslims

A large number of non-Muslims in practically all parts of the modern world are also eager to understand the message of the Quran. Such people would also find this book interesting and useful. It will enable them to understand the role of the Quran in transforming human character and personality.

*****

The ideal course is to allow the Message of the Quran to mould one's thoughts and behaviors during the early years of one's life. That is the surest safeguard against all possible going astray during later life.

Quranic guidance could also help an adult who may have missed the early opportunity to learn from it. It is never too late to learn the art of good living. From this point of view, *Quran for Children* could also serve a meaningful purpose for all shades and grades of people of the world. Any child and any adult, with or without previous knowledge of the Quran, could gain from its revolutionary message.

Life in the modern world has affected children in the worst way. The modern child finds himself or herself living in a world characterized by all sorts of strain and stress, tension and turmoil. Purposelessness, waywardness, crime and delinquency are on the increase. Life around us seems to have lost most of its charm. Some unwholesome development in the younger generation appears to be manifestly absurd. They are even suicidal for the human race. Such a contaminated atmosphere presents serious difficulties for all those forces which are working for the safety and betterment of children. The doors to survival and development often appear to be closed forever.

One of the best ways of facing the challenge of the time is to read and practice the Quran. Childhood is the right stage to start along the constructive path. This would be the healthiest way of keeping one's self unaffected by the undesirable trends and dangers of the age. There could be no better way of ensuring a safe march on the road to a wholesome and an all-round development.

Viewed against such a perspective, a study of this book and, through it of the Quran, is both pleasant as well as advantageous. It is a must for all such children and adults as are genuinely interested in sound growth and a proper refinement of human character and personality.

2
Who is God?

Section 1: Introduction

Who is God? How are we related to Him? What is the practical use of believing in God? This chapter presents a selection of some simple Quranic verses (sing. *āyah*, pl. *āyāt*) or Signs which throw light on the idea of God and His relation to people. There is no power greater than God. Right faith in God is necessary in order to develop character and personality. It promotes a peaceful and prosperous life. The verses selected for this chapter help in understanding the following ideas:

Section 2: God is One

God is One. He has no partner. He is Almighty.

Section 3: God's Bounties and Blessings

The entire universe is a manifestation of God's bounties and powers.

Section 4: God is Aware of Our Deeds

Our intentions and actions are fully known to him.

Section 5: God Helps Us

He who helps those who follow the right path and who work hard.

Section 6: Seek God's Help Alone

God alone can enable us to overcome our difficulties and troubles. We should ask for His help to succeed and for success in our efforts

Section 7: Conclusion

*****

Let's check what we have learned in

Section 1: Introduction:

Identification:

1. What is the Arabic word for verse and verses? What else does the word mean?

Clarification:

2. What five ways help us know that God loves and helps us according to the author?

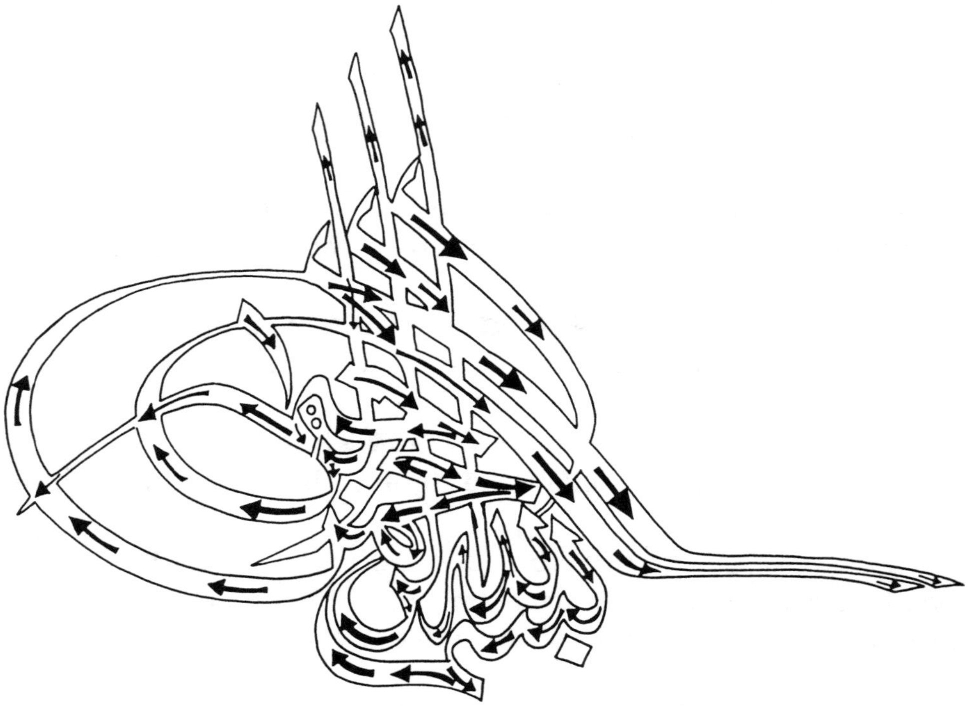

Section 2: God is One

1. Your God is One God (2:163).

ilāhukum ilāhuw-wāḥid

إِلَٰهُكُمْ إِلَٰهٌ وَٰحِدٌ

wāḥid	*ilāh*	*ilāhukum*
(is) One	God	your God (is)

2. He is the One God (112:1).

huwa-llāhu aḥad

هُوَ اللَّهُ أَحَدٌ

aḥad	*Allāh*	*huwa*
the One	the God	He is

3. God is All-powerful (2:109).

inna-llāha ᶜalā-kulli shayᵓin qadīr

إِنَّ اللَّهَ عَلَىٰ كُلِّ شَيْءٍ قَدِيرٌ

qadīr	*shayᵓin*	*kulli*	*ᶜalā*	*Allāh*	*inna*
Powerful	thing	every	over	God	(truly)

4. Truly God is Gentle and Compassionate to mankind (2:143).

inna-llāha bin-nāsi la-raᵓūfur raḥīm

إِنَّ اللَّهَ بِالنَّاسِ لَرَءُوفٌ رَّحِيمٌ

raḥīm	*la-raᵓūf*	*bin-nāsi*	*Allāh*	*inna*
Compassionate	Gentle(is)	to people	God	(truly)

5. God is the Lord of mighty Grace (2:105).

Allāh dhūl-faḍli-lᶜaẓīm

اللَّهُ ذُو الْفَضْلِ الْعَظِيمِ

al-ᶜaẓīm	*al-faḍl-*	*dhū*	*Allāh*
(the) mighty	(the) Grace	Lord of	God (is)

6. He is the Acceptor of Repentance; Compassionate (9:104).

huwat-tawwābur-raḥīm

هُوَ التَّوَّابُ الرَّحِيمُ

ar-raḥīm	*at-tawwāb*	*huwa*
the Compassionate	the Acceptor of Repentance	He (is)

7. He befriends the righteous (7:196).

huwa yatawallā-ṣ ṣāliḥīn

هُوَ يَتَوَلَّى الصّٰلِحِينَ

aṣ-ṣāliḥīn	*yatawallā*	*huwa*
the righteous	befriends	He

Let's find out what you have learned from

Section 2: God is One:

Identification:

1. All-powerful
2. The One God

Clarification:

3. Who accepts our repentance?
4. Who befriends those who do good?

Section 3: God's Bounties and Blessings

1. Whatever blessing you have, it is from God (16:53).

mā bikum min-ni^{c}mat fa-mina-llāh

مَا بِكُم مِّن نِّعْمَةٍ فَمِنَ اللّٰهِ

Allāh	*fa-min*	*ni^{c}matin*	*min*	*bikum*	*mā*
God	(it is) from	blessing	of	you have	whatever

2. Truly in the creation of the heavens and the earth

inna fī khalqis-samāwāti wa -l^{c}arḍ

إِنَّ فِي خَلْقِ السَّمٰوٰتِ وَ

al-^{c}arḍ	*wa*	*aṣ-ṣamāwāti*	*khalq*	*fī*	*inna*
the earth	and	the heavens	creation (of)	in	(truly)

and the alternation of night and day

wa-khtilāfil-layli wan-nahār

الْأَرْضِ وَاخْتِلٰفِ الَّيْلِ وَ النَّهَارِ

an-nahār	*wa*	*al-layli*	*ikhtilāfi*	*wa*
the day	and	night	alternation (of)	and

and the ship that runs in the sea with profit for people

wal-fulkil-latī tajrī fiḷ-baḥr bimā yanfa^c un-nās

وَ الْفُلْكِ الَّتِي تَجْرِي فِي الْبَحْرِ بِمَا يَنْفَعُ النَّاسَ

an-nās	*yanfa^c*	*bimā*	*al-baḥr*	*fī*	*allati*	*tajrī*	*al-fulk*
the people	profits	that which	sea	in	which	runs	the ship

and the water that God sends down from the heaven thereby reviving life

wa mā anzala-llāhu minas-samāʾi mim-māʾin fa-aḥyā

وَ مَآ أَنْزَلَ اللّٰهُ مِنَ السَّمَآءِ مِن مَّآءٍ فَأَحْيَا

fa-aḥyā	*māʾ*	*min*	*as-samāʾi*	*min-*	*Allāhu*	*anzal*	*ma*
then revived life	water	from	the sky	from	God	sent down	that which

with it to the earth after it is dead and His scattering

bihi-l-^{c}arḍ ba^{c}da mawtihā wa baththa

بِهِ الْأَرْضَ بَعْدَ مَوْتِهَا وَبَثَّ

baththa	*wa*	*mawtihā*	*ba^{c}da*	*al-^{c}arḍ*	*bihi*
dispersed	and	it is dead	after	the earth	with it

in it all kinds of animals, and the alteration of the winds

fīhā min kulli daābbatiw-wa taṣrīfi r-riyāḥi

فِيهَا مِن كُلِّ دَآبَّةٍ وَتَصْرِيفِ الرِّيٰحِ

ar-riyāḥ	*taṣrīf*	*wa*	*daābbat*	*kull*	*min*	*fīhā*
the winds	alteration	and	animals	all	of	in it

and the clouds spread between heaven and earth,

was-saḥābil musakhkhari bayn as-samā$^{\circ}$i wa-l-^{c}arḍ

وَالسَّحَابِ الْمُسَخَّرِ بَيْنَ السَّمَآءِ وَالْأَرْضِ

al-^{c}arḍ	*wa*	*as-samā$^{\circ}$*	*bayn*	*al-musakhkhari*	*as-saḥābil*	*wa*
the earth	and	heaven	between	spread	the clouds	and

there are the signs for a people who understand (2:164).

la-āyātil liqawmiy-ya^{c}qilūn

لَأٰيٰتٍ لِّقَوْمٍ يَعْقِلُونَ

ya^{c}qilūn	*liqawm*	*la-āyāti*
(who) understand	for a people (are)	indeed signs

3. Of His Signs is the creation of the heavens and the earth

min ayātihī khalqu s-samāwāti wa-l-^{c}arḍ

وَمِنْ ءَايٰتِهِ خَلْقُ السَّمٰوٰتِ وَالْأَرْضِ

al-^{c}arḍ	*wa*	*as-samāwāti*	*khalq*	*ayātihī*	*min*
the earth	and	the heavens	(is the)creation (of)	His Signs	of

and the diversity of your languages and your colors (30:22).

wa-khtilāfu alsinatikum wa alwānikum

وَٱخْتِلَٰفُ أَلْسِنَتِكُمْ وَأَلْوَٰنِكُمْ

alwānikum	*wa*	*alsinatikum*	*ikhtilāfu*	*wa*
your colors	and	your languages	(the) diversity (of)	and

4. If the sea were ink for the words of my Lord,

law kāna-l-baḥru midādal-likalimāti rabbī

لَّوْ كَانَ ٱلْبَحْرُ مِدَادًا لِّكَلِمَٰتِ رَبِّي

rabbī	*likalimāti*	*midādan*	*al-baḥr*	*kāna*	*law*
my Lord	for the words (of)	ink	the sea	were	if

the sea would surely be exhausted

la-nafida-l-baḥr

لَنَفِدَ ٱلْبَحْرُ

al-baḥr	*la-nafida-*
the sea	surely would be exhausted

before the words of my Lord are exhausted (18:109).

qabla an tanfada kalimātu rabbī

قَبْلَ أَن تَنفَدَ كَلِمَٰتُ رَبِّي

rabbī	*kalimāt*	*tanfada*	*qabla*	*an*
my Lord	words (of)	were exhausted	before	(that)

5. If all the trees on earth were pens and the sea (were ink)

law anna mā fil-ᶜarḍ min shajaratin aqlāmūw-wal-baḥr

لَوْ أَنَّمَا فِي ٱلْأَرْضِ مِن شَجَرَةٍ أَقْلَٰمٌ وَٱلْبَحْرُ

al-baḥr	*wa*	*aqlām*	*shajara*	*min*	*al-ᶜarḍ*	*fī*	*mā*	*law anna*
the sea	and	pens	tree (s)	of	the earth	on	whatever	if (were)

with seven seas more to help it

yamudduhu mim ba^{c}dihi sab^{c}atu abḥur

يَمُدُّهُۥ مِنۢ بَعْدِهِۦ سَبْعَةُ أَبْحُرٍ

abḥur	*sab^{c}atu*	*ba^{c}dihi*	*mim*	*yamudduhu*
seas	seven	beyond it	(from)	helps it

the words of God would not be exhausted (31:27).

mā nafidatu kalimāt ul-lāh

مَّا نَفِدَتْ كَلِمَٰتُ ٱللَّهِ

Allāh	*kalimāt*	*nafidatu*	*ma*
God	words of	would be exhausted	not

6. He gave you hearing, sight

ja^{c}ala lakumu s-sam^{c}a wal-abṣara

جَعَلَ لَكُمُ ٱلسَّمْعَ وَٱلْأَبْصَٰرَ

al-abṣar	*as-sam^{c}a*	*lakum*	*ja^{c}ala*
the sight	the hearing	for you	He made

and heart that you might thank Him (16:78).

wal-af$^{\circ}$idata la^{c}allakum tashkurūn

وَٱلْأَفْـِٔدَةَ لَعَلَّكُمْ تَشْكُرُونَ

tashkurūn	*la^{c}allakum*	*al-af$^{\circ}$ida*	*wa*
give thanks	so that you might	the hearts	and

Let's find out what you have learned from
Section 3: God's Bounties and Blessings:

Identification:

1. God's bounties listed in 16:53.
2. Trees as pens; sea as ink.

Clarification:

3. How is the diversity of our languages a Sign of God?
4. How are the colors of our skin a Sign of God?

Section 4: God is Aware of Our Deeds

1. God is aware of whatever you do (2:234).

allāhu bimā taʿmalūn khabīr

اللّٰهُ بِمَا تَعْمَلُونَ خَبِيرٌ

khabīr	*taʿmalūn*	*bimā*	*Allāh*
(is) aware	you do	with what	God

2. God is not unmindful of what you do (2:85).

mā-llahu bighāfilin ʿammā taʿmalūn

مَا اللّٰهُ بِغَٰفِلٍ عَمَّا تَعْمَلُونَ

taʿmalūn	*ʿammā*	*bighāfil*	*Allāh*	*mā*
you do	of what	unmindful	God	(is) not

3. Truly God knows what you do (16:91).

inna-llāha yaʿlamu mā tafʿalūn

إِنَّ اللّٰهَ يَعْلَمُ مَا تَفْعَلُونَ

tafʿalūn	*māy*	*aʿlam*	*Allāh*	*inna*
you do	what	knows	God	truly

4. He is with you wherever you may be (57:4).

huwa maʿakum ayna-mā kuntum

هُوَ مَعَكُمْ أَيْنَ مَا كُنتُمْ

kuntum	*ayna-mā*	*maʿakum*	*huwa*
you were	wherever	with you	He (is)

5. Truly nothing is hidden from God

inna-llāha lā yakhfā ʿalayhi shayʾun

إِنَّ اللّٰهَ لَا يَخْفَىٰ عَلَيْهِ شَيْءٌ

shayʾ	*ʿalayhi*	*yakhfā*	*lā*	*Allāh*	*inna*
anything	on Him	is hidden	not	God	truly

on earth or in the heavens (3:5).

fil-arḍ wa lā fī s-samāᵓi

فِي الْأَرْضِ وَلَا فِي السَّمَآءِ

as-samāᵓ	*fī*	*lā*	*wa*	*al-ᶜarḍ*	*fī*
the heavens	in	not	and	the earth	in

6. Whatever good you do, God knows it (2:197).

mā tafᶜalū min khayrī-yaᶜlamh ul-llāh

مَا تَفْعَلُوا مِنْ خَيْرٍ يَعْلَمْهُ اللَّهُ

Allāh	*yaᶜlamhu*	*khayr*	*min*	*tafᶜalū*	*mā*
God	knows it	good	of	you do	whatever

7. God knows what you conceal and what you reveal (16:19).

allāhu yaᶜlamu mā tusirrūn wa mā tuᶜlinūn

اللَّهُ يَعْلَمُ مَا تُسِرُّونَ وَمَا تُعْلِنُونَ

tuᶜlinūn	*mā*	*wa*	*tusirrūn*	*mā*	*yaᶜlamu*	*Allāh*
you reveal	what	and	you conceal	what	knows	God

8. God knows all that you reveal and that you conceal (7:99).

allāhu yaᶜlamu mā tubdūn wa mā taktumūn

اللَّهُ يَعْلَمُ مَا تُبْدُونَ وَمَا تَكْتُمُونَ

taktumūn	*wa*	*tubdūn*	*mā*	*yaᶜlam*	*Allāh*
you conceal what	and	you reveal	that	knows	God

9. He knows what you do secretly or openly. He knows what you earn (by your deeds) (6:3).

yaᶜlamu sirrakum wa jahrakum wa yaᶜlamu mā taksibūn

يَعْلَمُ سِرَّكُمْ وَجَهْرَكُمْ وَيَعْلَمُ مَا تَكْسِبُونَ

taksibūn	*mā*	*yaᶜlamu*	*wa*	*jahrakum*	*wa*	*sirrakum*	*yaᶜlamu*
you earn	what	He knows	and	your public act	and	your secret	He knows

10. Whether you hide your word or say it openly.

asirrū qawlakum awi-jharū bihi

أَسِرُّوا قَوْلَكُمْ أَوِ اجْهَرُوا بِهِ

bihi	*ijharū*	*aw*	*qawlakum*	*asirrū*
(with) it	declare	or	your speech	hide

He truly has knowledge of the secrets in the hearts (67:13).

innahu ʿalīm bidhāti ṣ-ṣudur

إِنَّهُ عَلِيمٌ بِذَاتِ الصُّدُورِ

aṣ-ṣudur	*bidhāt*	*ʿalīm*	*innahu*
(of) the hearts	of the essence	knowing	He truly (is)

11. Whether you reveal anything or conceal it,

in tubdū shayʾan aw tukhfūhu

إِنْ تُبْدُوا شَيْئًا أَوْ تُخْفُوهُ

tukhfūhu	*aw*	*shayʾ*	*tubdū*	*in*
you conceal it	or	thing	you reveal	if

truly God has knowledge of all things (33:54).

fa-inna-llāha kāna bikulli shayʾin ʿalīm

فَإِنَّ اللَّهَ كَانَ بِكُلِّ شَيْءٍ عَلِيمًا

ʿalīm	*shayʾin*	*bikulli*	*kāna*	*Allāh*	*fa-inna*
knowing	thing	of every	was	God	truly

12. Whether you show what is in your minds or

in tubdū mā fi anfusikum aw

إِنْ تُبْدُوا مَا فِي أَنْفُسِكُمْ أَوْ

aw	*anfusikum*	*fi*	*mā*	*tubdū*	*in*
or	your minds	in	what (is)	you show	whether

conceal it, God shall call you to account for it (2:284).

tukhfūhu yuḥāsibkum bihi-lāh

تُخْفُوهُ يُحَاسِبْكُم بِهِ اللهُ

Allāh	*bihi*	*yuḥāsibkum*	*tukhfūhu*
God	for it	shall call you to account	you conceal it

Let's find out what you have learned from

Section 4: God is Aware of Our Deeds:

Identification:

1. Who knows the good that we do?
2. Who knows what we conceal and what we reveal?

Clarification:

3. How does God know the secrets in our hearts?
4. Will God only call us to account for the deeds we do to each other?

Section 5: God Helps Us

1. God intends ease for you.

yurīdu-llāhu bikum ul-yusra

يُرِيدُ اللّٰهُ بِكُمُ الْيُسْرَ

al-yusr	*bikum Allāh*	*yurīd*
the ease	for you God	intends

He does not intend to put you to difficulties (2:185).

wa lā yurīdu bikum ul-^{c}usra

وَلَا يُرِيدُ بِكُمُ الْعُسْرَ

al-^{c}usr	*bikum*	*yurīd*	*lā*	*wa*
difficulty	for you	intends	not	and

2. He who fears God, (God) makes for him

may-yattaqi-llāha yaj^{c}al-lahu

مَنْ يَتَّقِ اللّٰهَ يَجْعَلْ لَهُ

lahu	*yaj^{c}al*	*Allāh*	*yattaqi*	*man*
for him	He makes	God	fears	he who

his path easy (65:4).

min amrihi yusran

مِنْ أَمْرِهِ يُسْرًا

yusran	*amrihi*	*min*
easy	his affair	of

3. I listen to the prayer of the petitioner

ujību da^{c}watad-dā^{c}i

أُجِيبُ دَعْوَةَ الدَّاعِ

ad-dā^{c}i	*da^{c}watu*	*ujīb*
the petitioner	(the) prayer (of)	I listen to

when he calls on Me (2:186).

idhā da^cāni

إِذَا دَعَانِ

da^{c}āni	*idhā*
he calls on Me	when

Let's check what we have learned in

Section 5: God Helps Us:

Identification:

1. The praying person
2. What do we do when we pray?

Clarification:

3. Does God say He wants to cause us difficulty?
4. When does God listen to our prayers?

Section 6: Seek God's Help Alone

1. Whoever holds firmly to God will be guided

may-ya^{c}taṣim billāhi faqad hudiya

مَنْ يَعْتَصِمْ بِاللَّهِ فَقَدْ هُدِيَ

hudiya	*faqad*	*billāh*	*ya^{c}taṣim*	*man*
will be guided	(he) has been	to God	holds firmly	whoever

to a right path (3:101).

ilā ṣiraṭim-mustaqīm

إِلَىٰ صِرَٰطٍ مُّسْتَقِيمٍ

mustaqīmin	*ṣiraṭin*	*ilā*
right	path	to

2. Thee do we worship and from Thee we seek help (1:4).

īyyāka na^{c}budu wa īyyāka nasta^{c}īn

إِيَّاكَ نَعْبُدُ وَإِيَّاكَ نَسْتَعِينُ

nasta^{c}īn	*īyāka*	*wa*	*na^{c}budu*	*īyāka*
we seek help from	Thee	and	we worship	Thee

3. When you have taken a decision, then trust in God.

fa-idhā ^{c}azamta fa-tawakkal ^{c}alā l-lāhi

فَإِذَا عَزَمْتَ فَتَوَكَّلْ عَلَى اللَّهِ

Allāh	*^{c}alā*	*fa-tawakkal*	*^{c}azamta*	*fa idhā*
God	on	then trust	you have taken a decision	and when

Truly God loves those who put their trust (in Him) (3:159).

inna-llāha yuḥibbu l-mutawakkilin

إِنَّ اللَّهَ يُحِبُّ الْمُتَوَكِّلِينَ

mutawakkilin	*yuḥibbu*	*Allāh*	*inna*
those who trust (Him)	loves	God	truly

4. If God helps you, none shall overpower you.

iy-yanṣurkumu-llāhu falā ghaliba lakum

إِن يَنصُرْكُمُ اللَّهُ فَلَا غَالِبَ لَكُمْ ج

ghaliba	*lakum*	*falā*	*Allāhu*	*yanṣurkum*	*in*
overcome	you	then none	God	helps you	if

If He forsakes you,

wa iy-yakhdhulkum

وَإِن يَخْذُلْكُمْ

yakhdhulkum	*in*	*wa*
He forsakes you	if	and

who is there, after that, who can help you (3:160).

fa-man dhāl-ladhī yanṣurukum mim ba^{c}dihi

فَمَن ذَا الَّذِي يَنصُرُكُم مِّن بَعْدِهِ

ba^{c}dihi	*mim*	*yanṣurukum*	*dhāl-ladhī*	*fa-man*
after that	(from)	helps you	(is) the possessor of that which one	then who

Let's find out what you have learned from

Section 6: Seek God's Help Alone:

Identification:

1. The Straight Path
2. Who do we worship and whose help alone do we seek?

Clarification:

3. Verse 3:159 tells us to make a decision and then trust in God. Explain what this means.
4. Explain verse 3:160 in your own words.

Section 7: Conclusion

We see that God loves us and helps us in various ways. We have learned verses that show us how loving of us God is, His bounties and blessings which are like infinite words and Signs to us of God's Presence in the universe. We learn that God is aware of our deeds whether they are open or hidden and that He alone helps us. Therefore, in loving God as God loves us, we seek God's help alone.

Section Answers

Section 1: Introduction

1. Verse refers to the Arabic word *ayah* which means sign.
2. Five ways that help us know that God loves us: Our loving God, God's Bounties and Blessings; God is Aware of our deeds; God helps us; seek God's help alone.

Section 2: Our Loving God

1. God.
2. God.
3. God.
4. God.

Section 3: God is Aware of Our Deeds

1. God's Bounties and Blessings listed in 16:53: Alternation of day and night; ships which sail; goods for profit; water from the ship; life on earth; animals; the changing winds; the clouds; heaven and earth.
2. If trees were pens, they would end before God's Words; if the seas were ink, they would end before God's Words.
3. They are a sign of God's Presence.
4. As Creator of the heavens and the earth.

Section 4: God is Aware of Our Deeds

1. God is Aware.
2. God is Aware.
3. God knows because God created Us.
4. No. God will also call us to account for what is in our minds.

Section 5: God Helps Us

1. A person who is praying to God.
2. Call on God.
3. No. God intends ease for those of us who guard against wrongdoing.
4. When we call on God.

Section 6: Seek God's Help Alone

1. For those who hold firmly to God.
2. God.
3. In 3:159, God is telling us to decide things for ourselves and once we have done so, to trust in God. This verse tells us that we are to decide to do our duty and leave the rest to God by trusting in God.
4. 3:16 means that God is All-powerful and if He helps us, no one can change the help He gives us. On the other hand, if He forsakes us, none can save us.

3
Islam and Muslims

Section 1: Introduction

What is Islam? Who are Muslims? Some selected Quranic verses are presented in this chapter which help in understanding the meaning of Islam and the character of Muslims. The Islamic way of life has been found to be the most constructive and the most creative. Islamic principles and practices have proven extremely beneficial for humanity. The Quranic verses offered in this chapter revolve around the following themes:

Section 2: A True and Wholesome Faith

Submission to God's (*islam*) will is the true religion. It is the most wholesome way of life.

Section 3: Our Book of Guidance

The Quran is the holy Book of Muslims. Its study promises health, happiness and success.

Section 4: Follow God and His Messenger

It is always beneficial to act on the commands of God and the teachings of His Messenger Muhammad (ﷺ).

Section 5: The Muslim Prescribed Prayer

Prayer is prescribed for Muslims. Prescribed prayer prevents wrongdoing.

Section 6: Life Has a Purpose

A Muslim is inspired by noble and creative ideals and tries not to lead a life without purpose.

Section 7: The Islamic Way of Life

Muslims focus on doing good. They avoid wrongdoing in all areas of their life.

Section 8: TheWorld's Best Citizens

Muslims should preach healthy ideas and practice good deeds.

Section 9: Conclusion

Let's find out what you have learned from

Section 1: Introduction

Identification:

1. What does Islam mean?
2. What does the Book of Guidance refer to?

Clarification:

3. What does "follow God and His Messenger" mean?
4. How is submission to God's will the true religion?

Section 2: A True and Wholesome Faith

1. Truly the true religion, according to God, is submission to God's Will (Islam) (3:19).

inna d-dīn ^{c}inda-llāhi l-islām

إِنَّ ٱلدِّينَ عِندَ ٱللَّهِ ٱلْإِسْلَٰمُ

al-islām	*Allāhi*	*^{c}inda*	*ad-dīn*	*inna*
(is) submission to God's Will (Islam)	God	with	the religion	truly

2. This day have I perfected for you your religion,

alyawm akmaltu lakum dīnakum

ٱلْيَوْمَ أَكْمَلْتُ لَكُمْ دِينَكُمْ

dīnakum	*lakum akmaltu*	*alyawm*
your religion	for you I have perfected	today

completed My blessings to you,

wa atmamtu ^{c}alaykum ni^{c}matī

وَأَتْمَمْتُ عَلَيْكُمْ نِعْمَتِي

ni^{c}matī	*^{c}alaykum*	*atmamtu*	*wa*
My blessings	on you	I have completed	and

and chosen for you submission to God's Will (Islam) as a religion (way of life) (5:3).

wa raḍītu lakumu l-islām dīnan

وَرَضِيتُ لَكُمُ ٱلْإِسْلَٰمَ دِينًا

dīnan	*al-islām*	*lakumu*	*raḍītu*	*wa*
as a religion	(the) Islam	for you	I have chosen	and

3. *Whoever seeks a religion other than submission to God's Will (Islam),*

may-yabtaghi ghayr al-islām dīnan

مَنْ يَبْتَغِ غَيْرَ الْإِسْلٰمِ دِينًا

dīnan	*al-islām*	*ghayr*	*yabtaghi*	*man*
as a religion	(the) Islam	other (than)	seeks	whoever

it shall not be accepted of him

fa-lay yuqbala minhu wa huwa

فَلَنْ يُقْبَلَ مِنْهُ ۚ وَهُوَ

huwa	*wa*	*minhu*	*yuqbala*	*fa-lan*
he (will be)	and	from him	be accepted	then it will not

and he shall be among the losers in the hereafter (3:85).

fil ākhira min al-khāsirīn

فِي الْأٰخِرَةِ مِنَ الْخٰسِرِينَ

al-khāsirīn	*min*	*ākhira*	*fī*
the losers	among	the hereafter	in

Let's find out what you have learned from

Section 2: A True and Wholesome Faith

1. What is the true religion?
2. The only religion accepted by God is?

Clarification:

3. Who will be among the losers?
4. Explain the difference between perfection and completion in your own words.

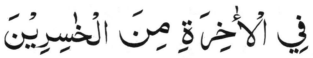

Section 3: Our Book of Guidance

1. This Book, about which there is no doubt, is a guidance

dhālik al-kitābu lā rayba fīhi

ذَٰلِكَ الْكِتَٰبُ لَا رَيْبَ ۛ فِيهِ

fīhi	*rayba*	*lā*	*al-kitāb*	*dhālik*
in it	doubt	no	the Book	that (is)

for the Godfearing(2:2).

hudā l-lilmuttaqīn

هُدًى لِّلْمُتَّقِينَ

lilmuttaqīn	*hudā*
for the Godfearing	a guidance

2. Truly this Quran guides to the Straight Path (17:9)

inna hādhā l-qurʾān yahdī l-lillatī hiya aqwam

إِنَّ هَٰذَا الْقُرْأَنَ يَهْدِي لِلَّتِي هِيَ أَقْوَمُ

aqwam	*hiya*	*l-lillatī*	*yahdī*	*al-qurʾān*	*hādhā*	*inna*
straightest	it (is)	unto that which	guides	(the) Quran	this	truly

3. When you read the Quran, seek refuge

fa-idhā qaraʾtal-qurʾan fa-staʿidh

فَإِذَا قَرَأْتَ الْقُرْأَنَ فَاسْتَعِذْ

fa-staʿidh	*al-qurʾan*	*qaraʾa*	*idhā*	*fa*
then seek refuge	the Quran	you read	when	so

with God from satan, the reviled (16:98).

billāhi min ash-shayṭān ir-rajīm

بِاللَّهِ مِنَ الشَّيْطَٰنِ الرَّجِيمِ

ar-rajīm	*ash-shayṭān*	*min*	*billāhi*
the reviled	(the) satan	from	with God

4. Recite so much of the Quran as is easy (for you) 73:20).

fa-qrāʾū mā tayassara min al-qurʾān

فَاقْرَءُوا مَا تَيَسَّرَ مِنَ الْقُرْآنِ

al-qurʾān	*min*	*tayassara*	*mā*	*fa-qrāʾū*
the Quran	from	is easy	what	so recite

5. Had We sent down this Quran on a mountain,

law anzalnā hādhāl-qurʾān ʿalā jabalil-

لَوْ أَنزَلْنَا هَٰذَا الْقُرْآنَ عَلَىٰ جَبَلٍ

jabalin	*ʿalā*	*al-qurʾān*	*hādhā*	*anzalnā*	*ḷaw*
a mountain	on	(the) Quran	this	We sent down	if

you would certainly have seen it falling down, splitting asunder

la-raaytahu khāshiʿam-mutaṣaddiʿam

لَّرَأَيْتَهُ خَاشِعًا مُّتَصَدِّعًا

mutaṣaddian	*khāshiʿan*	*la-raaytahu*
splitting asunder	falling down	you would certainly have seen it

because of the fear of God (59:21).

min khashyati-llāhi

مِّنْ خَشْيَةِ اللَّهِ

Allāh	*khashya*	*min*
God	fear (of)	from

Let's find out what we have learned from

Section 3: Our Book of Guidance:

Identification:

1. That which guides us to the Straight Path?
2. We seek refuge with God from whom?

Clarification:

3. Explain how the Quran takes us to the Straight Path.
4. Why is satan referred to as the damned?

Section 4: Follow God and His Messenger

1. Obey God and the Messenger so that you receive mercy (3:132).

aṭī^{c}ū llāha wa r-rasūla la^{c}allakum turhamūn

أَطِيعُوا اللَّهَ وَالرَّسُولَ لَعَلَّكُمْ تُرْحَمُونَ

turhamūn	*la^{c}allakum*	*ar-rasūl*	*wa*	*Allāh*	*aṭī^{c}ū*
receive mercy	so that you	the Messenger	and	God	obey

2. Whoever obeys God and His Messenger,

may-yuṭi^{c}i-llāha wa rasūlahu

مَنْ يُطِعِ اللَّهَ وَرَسُولَهُ

rasūlahu	*wa*	*Allāha*	*yuṭi^{c}i*	*man*
His Messenger	and	God	obeys	who

he indeed achieves a great success (33:71).

faqad fāza fawzan ^{c}aẓīman

فَقَدْ فَازَ فَوْزًا عَظِيمًا

^{c}aẓīman	*fawzan*	*fāza*	*faqad*
great	success	he has achieved	indeed

3. Whoever obeys God and His Messenger,

may-yuṭī^{c}u-llāha wa rasūlahu

مَنْ يُطِعِ اللَّهَ وَرَسُولَهُ

rasūlahu	*wa*	*Allāh*	*yuṭī^{c}*	*man*
His Messenger	and	God	obeys	whoever

fears God and does his duty towards (God) is

wa yakhsha-llāha wa yattaqhi

وَيَخْشَ اللَّهَ وَيَتَّقْهِ

yattaqhi	*wa*	*Allāh*	*yakhsha*	*wa*
fears Him	and	God	dreads	and

among the triumphant (24:52).

fa-ūlāʾika hum ul-fāʾizūn

فَأُولَٰٓئِكَ هُمُ الْفَآئِزُونَ

fāʾizūn	*hum*	*fa-ūlāʾika*
triumphant	they (are)	for those

4. O you who believe! Obey God and the Messenger

yā āyyuhal-ladhīna amanū aṭīʿū-llāha wa aṭīʿū r-rasūla

يَٰٓأَيُّهَا الَّذِينَ ءَامَنُوٓا أَطِيعُوا اللَّهَ وَأَطِيعُوا الرَّسُولَ

ar-rasūla	*aṭīʿū*	*wa*	*Allāh*	*aṭīʿū*	*amanū*	*ladhīna*	*āyyuha*	*yā*
the Messenger	obey	and	God	obey	believe	who	you	O

and do not make your deeds vain (47:33).

wa lā tubṭilū aʿmālakum

وَلَا تُبْطِلُوٓا أَعْمَٰلَكُمْ

aʿmālakum	*tubṭilū*	*lā*	*wa*
your deeds	make vain	not	and

5. Remember Me, I shall remember you.

fa-dhkurūnī adhkurkum

فَاذْكُرُونِيٓ أَذْكُرْكُمْ

adhkurkum	*fa-dhkurūnī*
I will remember you	so remember Me

And thank Me and do not deny Me (2:152).

wa-shkurū lī wa lā takfurūn

وَاشْكُرُوا لِي وَلَا تَكْفُرُونِ

takfurūn	*lā*	*wa*	*wa-shkurū lī*
deny Me	not	and	and thank Me

6. *Certainly you have in the Messenger of God a beautiful model (33:21).*

laqad kāna lakum fī rasūli-llāhi uswatun ḥasanatun

لَقَدْ كَانَ لَكُمْ فِي رَسُولِ اللَّهِ أُسْوَةٌ حَسَنَةٌ

ḥasanatun	*uswatun*	*Allāh*	*rasūli*	*fī*	*lakum*	*kāna*	*laqad*
(a) beautiful	a model	of God	Messenger	in	for you	was	certainly

7. *He is the Messenger of God and the seal of the prophets (33:40).*

wa lākir-rasūl-allāhi wa khātima n-nabiyīn

وَلَٰكِن رَّسُولَ اللَّهِ وَخَاتَمَ النَّبِيِّينَ

an-nabiyīn	*khātim*	*wa*	*Allāh*	*rasūl*	*wa*	*lākin*
the prophets	(the) seal (of)	and	(of) God	(the) Messenger	(and)	but (he is)

Let's find out what you have learned from

Section 4: Follow God and His Messenger:

Identification:

1. The Messenger to follow?
2. Who to remember?

Clarification:

3. Why are we told to obey God and His Messenger?
4. Who achieves success according to 33:71?

Section 5: The Muslim Prescribed Prayer

1. Truly prescribed prayer keeps (one) away from indecency

inna ṣ-ṣalāta tanhā ʿanil faḥshāʾi

إِنَّ ٱلصَّلَوٰةَ تَنْهَىٰ عَنِ ٱلْفَحْشَآءِ

faḥshāʾi	*ʿan*	*tanhā*	*aṣalāta*	*inna*
(the) indecency	(from)	prevents	the prescribed prayer	truly

and wrongdoing (29:45).

wa l-munkir

وَٱلْمُنكَرِ

al-munkir	*wa*
(the) wrongdoing	and

2. Keep up prescribed prayer, give the poor-due

aqīmūṣ-ṣalāta wa atū z-zakāta

أَقِيمُوا ٱلصَّلَوٰةَ وَءَاتُوا ٱلزَّكَوٰةَ

az-zakāta	*atū*	*wa*	*aṣ-ṣalāt*	*aqīmū*
poor-rate	give	and	(the) prayer	keep up

and bow down with those who bow (in prescribed prayer) (2:43).

wa arkaʿū maʿa r-rākiʿīn

وَٱرْكَعُوا مَعَ ٱلرَّٰكِعِينَ

ar-rākiʿīn	*maʿa*	*arkaʿu*	*wa*
those who bow	with	bow down	and

3. Oh you who believe! When the call

yā ayyuhā l-ladhīna āmanū idhā nūdiya

يَٰٓأَيُّهَا ٱلَّذِينَ ءَامَنُوٓا إِذَا نُودِيَ

nūdiya	*idhā*	*āmanū*	*al-ladhīna*	*yā ayyuhā*
the call is made	when	believe	who	O you

to the Friday prescribed prayer is made, then hasten

liṣṣalāti miy-yawmil-jumu^{c}ati fa-s^{c}ū

لِلصَّلٰوةِ مِنْ يَّوْمِ الْجُمُعَةِ فَاسْعَوْا

fa-s^{c}ū	*yawmil-jumu^{c}ah*	*min*	*liṣṣalāt*
then hasten	Friday	of	to the prescribed prayer

for the remembrance of God (62:9).

ilā dhikr-llāh

إِلٰى ذِكْرِ اللّٰهِ

Allāh	*dhikr*	*ilā*
(of) God	(the) remembrance	to

Let's find out what you have learned from

Section 5: The Muslim Prescribed Prayer:

Identification:

1. The beautiful model.

Clarification:

2. Prayer prevents what according to 29:45?
3. When to hasten for the remembrance of God according to 62:9?

Section 6: Life Has a Purpose

1. Do you imagine that We created you in vain (23:115)?

a-fa-ḥasibtum annamā khalaqnākum ᶜabathan

أَفَحَسِبْتُمْ أَنَّمَا خَلَقْنَٰكُمْ عَبَثًا

ᶜabathan	*khalaqnākum*	*innamā*	*fa-ḥasibtum*	*a*
in vain	We created you	that	do you think	?

2. We did indeed offer the Trust (responsibility)

innā ᶜaraḍnāl-amānata ᶜalā-

إِنَّا عَرَضْنَا ٱلْأَمَانَةَ عَلَى

ᶜalā	*al-amānata*	*araḍnā*	*innā*
to	the trust	We offered	truly

to the heavens, the earth and the mountains

-s-samāwāti wal-ᶜarḍ wal-jibāl

ٱلسَّمَٰوَٰتِ وَٱلْأَرْضِ وَٱلْجِبَالِ

al-jibāl	*wa*	*al-ᶜarḍ*	*wa -*	*as-samāwāti*
mountains	and	the earth	and	the heavens

but they refused to undertake it and were afraid of it.

fa-abayna ay-yaḥmilunahā wa ashfaquna

فَأَبَيْنَ أَن يَحْمِلْنَهَا وَأَشْفَقْنَ

ashfaquna	*wa*	*yaḥmilunah*	*an*	*fa-abayna*
were afraid	and	bear it	to	but they declined

The human being took it (the burden) (33:72).

minhā wa ḥamalahāl-insān

مِنْهَا وَحَمَلَهَا ٱلْإِنسَٰنُ

insān	*ḥamalahā*	*wa*	*minhā*
human being	took it (the burden)	and	of it

Let's find out what you have learned from

Section 6: Life Has a Purpose:

Identification:

1. To what does the Trust refer?
2. Who accepted the Trust?

Clarification:

3. Did God create us in vain according to 23:115?
4. Who refused the Trust?

Section 7: The Islamic Way of Life

1. The servants of the Compassionate are those who walk

^{c}ibādur-raḥmānil-ladhīna yamshūna

عِبَادُ الرَّحْمٰنِ الَّذِينَ يَمْشُونَ

yamshūn	*al-ladhīna*	*ar-raḥmān*	*^{c}ibād*
walk	(are) those who	the Compassionate	the worshippers (of)

upon the earth in humility.

^{c}alāl-^{c}arḍ hawnaw-

عَلَى الْأَرْضِ هَوْنًا

hawnan	*al-^{c}arḍ*	*^{c}alā*
humbly	the earth	on

When the ignorant address them, they say, 'Peace'.

wa idhā khāṭabahumu-l-jāhilūn qālū salāman

وَإِذَا خَاطَبَهُمُ الْجٰهِلُونَ قَالُوا سَلٰمًا

salāman	*qālū*	*al-jāhilūn*	*khāṭabahumu*	*idhā*	*wa*
peace	they would say	the ignorant	address them	when	and

They pass the night with their Lord, prostrate and standing up.

wa-lladhīna yabītūna lir-rabbihim sujjadaw-wa qiyāman wa-lladhīna

وَالَّذِينَ يَبِيتُونَ لِرَبِّهِمْ سُجَّدًا وَقِيٰمًا ۝ وَالَّذِينَ

al-ladhīna	*wa*	*qiyāman-*	*wa*	*sujjadan*	*lirabbihim*	*yabītūna*
those who	and	standing	and	in prostration	for their Lord	pass the night

They say, 'Our Lord! Avert from us

yaqūlūna rabbanā-ṣrif ^{c}annā

يَقُولُونَ رَبَّنَا اصْرِفْ عَنَّا

^{c}annā	*iṣrif*	*rabbanā*	*yaqūlūna*
from us	avert	our Lord	they say

the torment of hell for its torment is to perish;

ᶜadhāba jahannama inna ᶜadhabahā

عَذَابَ جَهَنَّمَ ۖ إِنَّ عَذَابَهَا

ᶜadhabahā	*inna*	*jahannama*	*ᶜadhāba*
its torment	truly	of hell	(the) torment

indeed it is an evil abode and station'.

kāna gharāman innahā saāᵓat mustaqarraq-wa-muqāman

كَانَ غَرَامًا ۖ إِنَّهَا سَاءَتْ مُسْتَقَرًّا وَمُقَامًا

muqāman	*wa*	*mustaqarran*	*saāᵓat*	*innahā*	*gharām*	*kāna*
station	and	abode	evil	truly it (is)	a penalty	would be

When they spend they are neither extravagant nor stingy.

wa-lladhīna idhā anfaqū lam yusrifū wa lam yaqtarū

وَالَّذِينَ إِذَا أَنفَقُوا لَمْ يُسْرِفُوا وَلَمْ يَقْتُرُوا

yaqtarū	*wa-lam*	*lam yusrifū*	*anfaqū*	*idhā*	*wa lladhīna*
be stingy	and not	would not be extravagant	they spend	when	and those who

They hold a balance in between those (extremes) (25:63-67).

wa kāna bayna dhāḷika qawāman

وَكَانَ بَيْنَ ذَٰلِكَ قَوَامًا

qawāman	*dhāḷika*	*bayna*	*kāna*	*wa*
a balance	those	between	would be	and

Let's find out what you have learned from

Section 7: The Islamic Way of Life:

Identification:

1. Those who walk on the earth with humility are?
2. Those who say, "Peace," (*salam*) to the ignorant?

Clarification:

3. What does it mean in verses 25:63-67 where the Quran says to neither be extravagant nor stingy?
4. How do those who walk on the earth with humility pass the night?

Section 8: The World's Best Citizens

1. You are the best Community ever sent forth

kuntum khayra ummatin ukhrijatu

كُنتُمْ خَيْرَ أُمَّةٍ أُخْرِجَتْ

ukhrijatu	*ummah*	*khayr*	*kuntum*
sent forth	Community	the best	you were

You enjoin humanity to the righteous act

lin-nās taʾmurūna bil-maʿruf

لِلنَّاسِ تَأْمُرُونَ بِالْمَعْرُوفِ

bil-maʿruf	*taʾmurūn*	*lin-nās*
to the righteous act	you enjoin	humanity

and forbid the wrong.

wa tanhawna ʿanil-munkar wa

وَتَنْهَوْنَ عَنِ الْمُنكَرِ وَ

wa	*munkar*	*ʿan*	*tanhawna*	*wa*
and	wrong	(from)	forbid	and

You believe in God (3:110).

tuʾminūna bil-lāh

تُؤْمِنُونَ بِاللَّهِ

bil-lāh	*tuʾminūn*
in God	you believe

2. Truly those who believe

innā-lladhīna āmanū

إِنَّ الَّذِينَ آمَنُوا

āmanū	*al-ladhīna*	*innā*
who believe	those who	truly

and do righteous deeds are the best of creatures (98:7).

wa ʿamalūṣ-ṣāliḥāt ūlāʾika hum khayrul-barrīyati

وَعَمِلُوا الصَّٰلِحَٰتِ أُوْلَٰٓئِكَ هُمْ خَيْرُ الْبَرِيَّةِ

barrīyati	*khayr*	*hum*	*ūlāʾika*	*aṣ-ṣāliḥā*	*ʿamalū*
(of) creatures	(the) best	they (are)those		(the) good deeds	they did

3. Be not weary nor cry out for peace.

fa-lā tahinū wa tadʿū ilā-s-salm

فَلَا تَهِنُوا وَتَدْعُوٓا إِلَى السَّلْمِ

as-salm	*ilā*	*tadʿū*	*wa*	*tahinū*	*fa-lā*
(the) peace	for	cry out	and	be weary	so not

You shall be triumphant (47:35).

wa antumul-āʿlūn

وَأَنْتُمُ الْأَعْلَوْنَ

al-āʿlūn	*antum*	*wa*
the uppermost	you (shall be)	and

4. Truly believers are a single brethren

innamāl-muʾminūn ikhwatun

إِنَّمَا الْمُؤْمِنُونَ إِخْوَةٌ

ikhwah	*al-muʾminūn*	*innamā*
are brethren	the believers	truly

so make reconciliation between your brothers (49:10).

fa-aṣliḥū bayna akhawaykum

فَأَصْلِحُوا بَيْنَ أَخَوَيْكُمْ

akhawaykum	*bayn*	*fa-aṣliḥū*
your brothers	between	so make reconciliation

5. Muhammad is the Messenger of God. Those who are with him

muḥammadur-rasūlu-llāh wa-lladhīna maᶜahū

مُحَمَّدٌ رَّسُولُ اللّٰهِ ط وَ الَّذِينَ مَعَهٗ

maᶜahū	al-ladhīna	wa	Allāh	rasūl	muḥammad
with him (are)	those who (are)	and	(of) God	(the) Messenger	Muhammad (is)

are firm against the unbelievers,

ashiddāᵓu ᶜalāl-kuffār

أَشِدَّآءُ عَلَى الْكُفَّارِ

al-kuffār	ᶜalā	ashiddāᵓ
unbelievers	against	firm

compassionate amongst themselves (48:29).

ruḥamāᵓu baynahum

رُحَمَآءُ بَينَهُمْ

baynahum	ruḥamāᵓu
among them	compassionate

Let's find out what you have learned from

Section 8: The World's Best Citizens:

Identification:
1. The best people according to 3:110 are?
2. The best people according to 98:7 are?

Clarification:
3. Explain in your own words
how you can be firm with unbelievers.
4. Explain in your own words
how you can be compassionate to each other as believers.

Section 9: Conclusion

We have come a long way in Chapter 3 towards understanding what it means to be among those who submit to God's Will (*muslim*) and what it means to follow submission to the Will of God *(islam)*. We now know that we have a true and wholesome or holistic faith. We are guided by the Quran which asks us to follow God and His Messenger. God has asked us to perform the prescribed prayer which helps us remember that life has a purpose. The purpose is to freely choose to submit to God's Will and in doing so, become among the world's best citizens.

Section Answers:

Section 1: Introduction

1. Submission to the Will of God.
2. The Quran.
3. It means to follow God's command, one of which is to model our lives on the life of the Messenger.
4. This is the way God creates us and it is, therefore, the most natural way. When each of us follow our own desires, the world becomes a place of chaos like it is today. When each of us follows God's Will and submit to it, the world becomes a place of order and harmony.

Section 2: A True and Wholesome Faith

1. Submission to the Will of God (*islam*).
2. Submission to the Will of God (*islam*).
3. Those who accept a religion other than submission to God's will.
4. God perfected His religion with the Quran and completed it with His Last Messenger.

Section 3: Our Book of Guidance

1. The Quran.
2. Satan.
3. By acting as our guide.
4. Because satan rebelled against God's Will by not bowing down before Adam as the angels did when they were asked to do this by God.

Section 4: Follow God and His Messenger

1. Muhammad (ﷺ).
2. God.
3. To be shown mercy.
4. Whoever obeys God and His Messenger.

Section 5: The Muslim Prescribed Prayer

1. Prophet Muhammad (ﷺ).
2. Indecency and wrongdoing.
3. When we hear the call of the Friday prescribed prayer.

Section 6: Life Has A Purpose

1. The Trust refers to being responsible to God for nature.
2. All human beings.
3. No, but some people imagine this to be so.
4. The heavens, earth and mountains.

Section 7: The Islamic Way of Life

1. The servants of God.
2. Those who walk on the earth with humility.
3. It means to follow the middle way, the Straight Path.
4. Standing and prostrating in prescribed prayer.

Section 8: The World's Best Citizens

1. Those who counsel to the positive and try to prevent the development of the negative.
2. Those who believe in God and do good deeds.
3. The best way to be firm is to not follow their way but set an example for them to also try to be the best people.
4. There are many ways and many examples. One important way is to remember the Sacred Tradition (*hadith qudsi*) of God where He said, "My mercy precedes My anger."

4
Fruits of Moral Behavior

Section 1: Introduction

What is moral behavior? Why should a child have good manners? This chapter offers some beautiful Quranic Signs which highlight constructive ways of thinking and moral and ethical styles of behaving. These Signs or verses are a stimulating source for child guidance. They possess special powers to improve children's character and personality. These easy to understand verses are presented under the following headings:

Section 2: Reward for Good Deeds

Moral behavior is rewarded in the present and the future life.

Section 3: Moral Behavior is Beneficial

It is to our advantage to live as good, moral human beings.

Section 4: Piety and Fear of God

Virtuous conduct and guarding against evil promotes a positive life-style, one that pleases God.

Section 5: Attitude Towards Parents

Our attitude towards our father and mother should be one of love, respect and service.

Section 6: Courtesy and Human Relations

All people living in our surroundings deserve appropriate courtesy.

Section 7: Why be good?

Goodness leads to a positive and successful life in both this world and the next.

Section 8: Charms of Everyday Conversation

Our daily conversation must reflect warmth, beauty, decency and grace.

Section 9: The Value of Truth

Truthfulness is helpful for successful living.

Section 10: Keep Your Promises!

Keeping our promises has great value in the Islamic way of life.

Section 11: Patience and Perseverance

A good child must exercise patience and steadfastness. These are character-building, positive virtues.

Section 12: The Harvest of Hard Work

Good, regular hard work always yields a rich harvest.

Section 13: Good Table Manners

Good eating and drinking habits add respect to human life.

Section 14: Personal Health and Hygiene

Cleanliness of the body and dress is essential for a positive and successful life.

Section 15: Forgiveness and Forbearance

Moral life demands forgiving people. We should try to overlook the errors and shortcomings of others.

Section 16: Friendship and Co-operation

A Muslim must consider all of humanity as a united brotherhood and sisterhood.

Section 17: Islamic Social Etiquette

Islamic social manners are most healthy. They are the key to successful living anywhere in the world.

Section 18: Conclusion

Let's find out what you have learned from
Section 1: Introduction:

Fill in the Blanks:

1. Patience and perseverance are ______________.
2. Moral life demands _________________.

Clarification:

3. Explain three of the fruits gained through moral behavior.
4. Explain how friendship and cooperation work.

Section 2: Reward for Good Deeds

1. Everyone will be paid in full (the fruit) of his deeds (39:70).

wuffiyat kullu nafsim-mā ᶜamilat

وُفِّيَتْ كُلُّ نَفْسٍ مَّا عَمِلَتْ

ᶜamilat	*mā*	*nafs*	*kull*	*wuffiyat*
(it) has done	what	soul	every	is paid in full

2. Whoever believes and performs

man āmana wa ᶜamila

مَنْ ءَامَنَ وَ عَمِلَ

ᶜamila	*wa*	*āmana*	*man*
performs	and	believes	whoever

righteousness shall have a goodly reward (18:88).

ṣāliḥan fa-lahu jazāᵓanil-ḥusnā

صَٰلِحًا فَلَهُۥ جَزَآءً ٱلْحُسْنَىٰ

jazāᵓanil-ḥusnā	*fa-lahu*	*ṣāliḥan*
goodly wage	indeed for him	righteousness

3. Those who believe and perform good deeds,

al-ladhīna āmanū wa ᶜamilūṣ-ṣāliḥāt

ٱلَّذِينَ ءَامَنُوا۟ وَ عَمِلُوا۟ ٱلصَّٰلِحَٰتِ

aṣ-ṣāliḥāt	*ᶜamilū*	*wa*	*āmanū*	*al-ladhīna*
(the) good deeds	perform	and	believe	those who

He will give them their wages abundantly

fa-yuwaffīhim ujūrahum wa

فَيُوَفِّيهِمْ أُجُورَهُمْ وَ

wa	*ujūrahum*	*fa-yuwaffīhim*
and	their wages then	He will give abundantly to them

and will increase His grace to them (4:173).

yazīduhum min faḍlihi

يَزِيدُهُمْ مِّنْ فَضْلِهِ

faḍlihi	min	yazīduhum
His grace	of	He will increase to them

4. God has promised those who believe

waʿada-llāhul-ladhīna āmanū

وَعَدَ اللهُ الَّذِينَ أَمَنُوْا

āmanū	al-ladhīna	Allāh	waʿada
believed	those who	God	promised

and do good deeds forgiveness and a great reward (5:9).

wa ʿamilūṣ-ṣāliḥāt lahum maghfiratuw- wa ajrun ʿaẓīmun

وَعَمِلُوا الصَّلِحَٰتِ لَهُمْ مَغْفِرَةٌ وَّأَجْرٌ عَظِيمٌ

ʿaẓīm	ajrun	wa	maghfiratun	lahum	aṣ ṣāliḥāt	ʿamilū
great	reward	and	forgiveness	for them	(the) good deeds	performed

5. For those who believe and work righteously

al-ladhīna āmanū wa ʿamilūṣ ṣāliḥāt

أَلَّذِينَ أَمَنُوْا وَعَمِلُوا الصَّلِحَٰتِ

aṣ ṣāliḥāt	ʿamilū	wa	āmanū	al-ladhīna
(the) good deeds	performed	and	believed	those who

is a bliss and a lovely resort (13:29).

ṭūbā lahum wa ḥusnu maābin

طُوبَىٰ لَهُمْ وَحُسْنُ مَأْبٍ

maābin	ḥusnu	wa	lahum	ṭūbā
resort	(of) beauty	and	for them	bliss

6. Whoever does good deeds, whether male or female

man ʿamila ṣaliḥam-min dhakarin aw unthā

مَنْ عَمِلَ صَٰلِحًا مِّن ذَكَرٍ أَوْ أُنثَىٰ

unthā	*aw*	*dhakar*	*min*	*ṣaliḥan*	*ʿamila*	*man*
female	or	male	from	a good deed	performed	who

and is a Believer, We will make them live

wa huwa muʾmin fa-la-nuḥyayannahu

وَهُوَ مُؤْمِنٌ فَلَنُحْيِيَنَّهُۥ

fa-la-nuḥyayannahu	*muʾmin*	*huwa*	*wa*
then We shall indeed renew his life	a believer	he (is)	and

an agreeable life and We shall indeed recompense them

ḥayātan ṭayyiban wa la-najziyannahum

حَيَوٰةً طَيِّبَةً ۖ وَلَنَجْزِيَنَّهُمْ

la-najziyannahum	*wa*	*ṭayyiban*	*ḥayātan*
We shall indeed recompense them	and	agreeable	a life

for the best of their actions (16:97).

ajrahum bi-aḥsani mā kānū yaʿmalūn

أَجْرَهُم بِأَحْسَنِ مَا كَانُوا۟ يَعْمَلُونَ

kānū yaʿmalūn	*mā*	*bi-aḥsani*	*ajrahum*
they used to do	that which	to the best (of)	their wage

7. Those who believe and do righteous deeds—

al-ladhīna āmanū wa ʿamilūṣ ṣāliḥat

ٱلَّذِينَ ءَامَنُوا۟ وَعَمِلُوا۟ ٱلصَّٰلِحَٰتِ

aṣ ṣāliḥat	*ʿamilū*	*wa*	*āmanū*	*al-ladhīna*
(the) good deeds	performed	and	believed	those who

Truly We shall not waste the reward of their good work (18:30).

innā lā nuḍiᶜ ajra man aḥsana ᶜamalan

إِنَّا لَا نُضِيعُ أَجْرَ مَنْ أَحْسَنَ عَمَلًا

ᶜamalan	aḥsa	man	ajr	nuḍiᶜ	lā	innā
in work	better	one who (is)	reward (of)	waste	not	truly We

8. Those who believe and perform good deeds

al-ladhīna āmanū wa ᶜamilūṣ-ṣāliḥat

الَّذِينَ أَمَنُوا وَعَمِلُوا الصَّلِحَتِ

aṣ-ṣāliḥat	ᶜamilū	wa	āmanū	al-ladhīna
(the) good deeds	do	and	believed	those who

We shall indeed grant pardon to them for their misdeeds and

la-nukaffiranna ᶜanhum sayyātihim wa

لَنُكَفِّرَنَّ عَنْهُمْ سَيِّأَتِهِمْ وَ

wa	sayyātihim	ᶜanhum	la-nukaffiranna
and	(for) their misdeeds	to them	We shall indeed grant pardon

shall reward them according to the best of their deeds (29:7).

la-najziyannahum aḥsanal-ladhī kānū-yaᶜmilūn

لَنَجْزِيَنَّهُمْ أَحْسَنَ الَّذِي كَانُوا يَعْمَلُونَ

kānū-yaᶜmilūn	al-ladhī	aḥsana	la-najziyannahum
they have been doing	that which	the best (of)	then We shall indeed compensate

9. For those who believe and do good deeds

al-ladhīna āmanū wa ᶜamilūṣ-ṣāliḥāt

الَّذِينَ أَمَنُوا وَعَمِلُوا الصَّلِحَتِ

aṣ-ṣāliḥāt	ᶜamilū	wa	āmanū	al-ladhīna
(the) good deeds	performed	and	believed	those who

is forgiveness and a magnificent reward (35:7).

lahum maghfiratuw-wa ajrun kabirun

لَهُم مَّغْفِرَةٌ وَأَجْرٌ كَبِيرٌ

kabirun	*ajrun*	*wa*	*maghfiratun*	*lahum*
magnificen	reward	and	forgiveness	for them

10. Those who believe and do good deeds,

al-ladhīna āmanū wa ᶜamilūṣ-ṣāliḥāt

الَّذِينَ آمَنُوا وَعَمِلُوا الصَّالِحَاتِ

aṣ-ṣāliḥāt	*ᶜamilū*	*wa*	*āmanū*	*al-ladhīna*
(the) good deeds	performed	and	believed	those who

their Lord will admit them to His Mercy.

fa-yudkhiluhum rabbuhum fī raḥmatihi

فَيُدْخِلُهُمْ رَبُّهُمْ فِي رَحْمَتِهِ ۚ

raḥmatihi	*fī*	*rabbuhum*	*fa-yudkhiluhum*
His Mercy	in	their Lord	then (He) will enter them

That is a clear triumph (45:30).

dhālika huwal-fawzu-l-mubin

ذَٰلِكَ هُوَ الْفَوْزُ الْمُبِينُ

al-mubin	*al-fawz*	*huwa*	*dhālika*
(the) clear	the triumph	it (is)	that

11. Those who believe, perform good deeds

al-ladhīna āmanū wa ᶜamilūṣ-ṣāliḥāt

الَّذِينَ آمَنُوا وَعَمِلُوا الصَّالِحَاتِ

aṣ-ṣāliḥāt	*ᶜamilū*	*wa*	*āmanū*	*al-ladhīna*
(the) good deeds	performed	and	believed	those who

and believe in what has been revealed to Muhammad

wa āmanū bimā nuzzila ʿalā muḥammad

وَأُمِنُوْا بِمَا نُزِّلَ عَلٰى مُحَمَّدٍ

muḥammad	ʿalā	nuzzila	bimā	āmanū	wa
Muhammad	on	was revealed	in what	believed	and

—and it is the truth from their Lord—

wa huwal-ḥaqqu mir-rabbihim

وَّهُوَ الْحَقُّ مِن رَّبِّهِمْ

rabbihim	min	al-ḥaqq	huwa	wa
their Lord	from	the truth	it (is)	and

He will forgive their misdeeds and restore their state (47:2).

kaffara ʿanhum sayyātihim wa aṣlaḥa bālahum

كَفَّرَ عَنْهُمْ سَيِّأتِهِمْ وَأَصْلَحَ بَالَهُمْ

bālahum	aṣlaḥa	wa	sayyātihim	ʿanhum	kaffara
their state	restored	and	their misdeeds	of them	He forgave

12. Whoever performs the weight of a speck of dust in goodness shall see it (99:7).

may-yaʿmalu mithqāla dharratin khayray-yarahu

مَنْ يَّعْمَلْ مِثْقَالَ ذَرَّةٍ خَيْرًا يَّرَهُ

yarahu	khayran	dharratin	mithqāla	yaʿmalu	man
shall see it	in goodness	a speck of dust	(the) weight (of)	performs	whoever

13. Those who believe and perform good deeds,

al-ladhīna āmanū wa ʿamilūṣ-ṣāliḥāt

الَّذِيْنَ أُمِنُوْا وَعَمِلُوا الصَّلِحٰتِ

aṣ-ṣāliḥāt	ʿamilū	wa	āmanū	al-ladhīna
(the) good deeds	performed	and	believed	those who

they will be the companions of paradise

ūlāʾika aṣḥabu-l-jannati

أُولَٰٓئِكَ أَصْحَٰبُ ٱلْجَنَّةِ ۖ

al-jannati	*aṣḥabu*	*ūlāʾika*
(the) paradise	(the) companions (of)	they (will be)

abiding in it forever (2:82).

hum fīhā khālidūn

هُمْ فِيهَا خَٰلِدُونَ

khālidūn	*fīhā*	*hum*
abiding forever	in it	they (are)

14. Whoever intercedes with a goodly recommendation

may-yashfaʿ shafāʿatan ḥasanatay-

مَّن يَشْفَعْ شَفَٰعَةً حَسَنَةً

ḥasanatan	*shafāʿatan*	*yashfaʿ*	*man*
goodly	an intercession	intercedes	whoever

there shall be a portion of it for him (4:85).

yakul-lahu naṣībum minhā

يَكُن لَّهُۥ نَصِيبٌ مِّنْهَا

minhā	*naṣībum*	*lahu*	*yakun*
of it	a portion	for him	(there) shall be

15. Whoever produces a good act there is for him a good from it (28:84).

man jāa bil-ḥasanati fa-lahu khayrum-minhā

مَن جَآءَ بِٱلْحَسَنَةِ فَلَهُۥ خَيْرٌ مِّنْهَا

minhā	*khayrun*	*fa-lahu*	*bil-ḥasanati*	*jāa*	*man*
from it	a good	then for him	a good act	produces	whoever

16. *Repel evil with that which is better than it (23:96).*

idfa^c bil-latī hiya aḥsanus-sayyi$^{\circ}$ati

إِدْفَعْ بِالَّتِي هِيَ أَحْسَنُ السَّيِّئَةَ

as-sayyi$^{\circ}$ati	*aḥsan*	*hiya*	*bil-latī*	*idfa^c*
evil	better (than)	it (is)	with that	repel

17. *The good act and the bad act are not equal. Repel the bad with what is better;*

lā tastawīl-ḥasanatu wa lās-sayyi$^{\circ}$atu idfa^c bil-latī hiya aḥsanu

لَا تَسْتَوِي الْحَسَنَةُ وَلَا السَّيِّئَةُ ط إِدْفَعْ بِالَّتِي هِيَ أَحْسَنُ

aḥsan	*hiya*	*bil-latī*	*idfa^c*	*as-sayyi$^{\circ}$atu*	*lā*	*wa*	*al-ḥasanatu*	*tastawī*	*lā*
better	it (is)	with that	repel	the bad	not	and	the good act	be equal	not

for then between you and him with whom there was enmity, it would be

fa-idhā-l-ladhī baynaka wa baynahu ^{c}adāwatun

فَإِذَا الَّذِي بَيْنَكَ وَبَيْنَهُ عَدَاوَةٌ

^{c}adāwatun	*baynahu*	*wa*	*baynaka*	*al-ladhī*	*fa-idhā*
(there is) enmity	between him	and	between you	he who	for then

as though he were a warm friend (41:34).

kannahu walīyun ḥamīm

كَأَنَّهُ وَلِيٌّ حَمِيمٌ

ḥamīm	*walīyun*	*kannahu*
warm	a friend	it were as though he

18. *The blind and the seeing are not equal,*

mā yastawil-^{c}amā wal-baṣīr

مَا يَسْتَوِي الْأَعْمَىٰ وَالْبَصِيرُ

al-baṣīr	*wa*	*al-^{c}amā*	*yastawi*	*mā*
the seeing	and	the blind	be equal	not

nor are those who believe and perform

wal-ladhīna āmanū wa ᶜamilū

وَالَّذِينَ ءَامَنُوا وَعَمِلُوا

ᶜamilū	*wa*	*āmanū*	*al-ladhīna*	*wa*
performed	and	believed	those who	and

good deeds and the evil-doer (40:58).

-ṣ-ṣāliḥāt wa lā l-musīᵓu

الصَّٰلِحَٰتِ وَلَا الْمُسِيٓءُ

al-musīᵓu	*lā*	*wa*	*aṣ-ṣāliḥāt*
the evil-doer	not	and	(the) good deeds

19. By the Tme! Truly the human being is at a loss

wal-ᶜaṣr innal-insāna la-fī khusrin

وَالْعَصْرِ ۝ إِنَّ الْإِنسَٰنَ لَفِي خُسْرٍ

khusrin	*la-fī*	*al-insān*	*inna*	*al-ᶜaṣri*	*wa*
a loss	indeed (he is) in	(the) human being	truly	the epoch	by

except those who have believed and have performed good deeds

illāl-ladhīna āmanū wa ᶜamilūṣ-ṣāliḥāt

إِلَّا الَّذِينَ ءَامَنُوا وَعَمِلُوا الصَّٰلِحَٰتِ

aṣ-ṣāliḥāt	*ᶜamilū*	*wa*	*āmanū*	*al-ladhīna*	*illā*
(the) good deeds	have performed	and	have believed	those who	except

and enjoin each other with the truth and

wa tawāṣaw bil-ḥaqq wa

وَتَوَاصَوْا بِالْحَقِّ ۙ وَ

wa	*bil-ḥaqq*	*tawāṣaw*	*wa*
and	(with) the truth	enjoin each other	and

enjoin patience on each other (103:1-3).

tawāṣaw biṣ-ṣabr

تَوَاصَوْا بِالصَّبْرِ

biṣ-ṣabr	*tawāṣaw*
with (the) patience	enjoin each other

Let's find out what you have learned from

Section 2: Reward for Good Deeds:

Fill in the blanks:

1. Reward is for ____________.
2. Surely the human being is at a loss except for those who ____________.

Clarification:

3. Who will pay our wages for our good deeds?
4. Who has God promised to forgive according to 5:9?

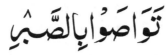

Section 3: Moral Behavior is Beneficial

1. Lo! Whoever performed a good deed, it is for himself

man ʿamila ṣāliḥan fa-linafsihi

مَنْ عَمِلَ صَٰلِحًا فَلِنَفْسِهِۦ

fa-linafsihi	*ṣāliḥan*	*ʿamila*	*man*
lo! (it is) for himself	a good deed	performed	whoever

and whoever does wrong it is against himself (41:46).

wa man asāʾa fa-ʿalayhā

وَمَنْ أَسَآءَ فَعَلَيْهَا

fa-ʿalayhā	*asāʾa*	*man*	*wa*
lo! (it is) against (his soul)	did evil	whoever	and

2. If you do good, you do it for yourselves.

in aḥsantum aḥsantum li-anfusikum

إِنْ أَحْسَنتُمْ أَحْسَنتُمْ لِأَنفُسِكُمْ

li-anfusikuma	*ḥsantum*	*aḥsantum*	*in*
for yourselves	you did good	you did good	if

If you do wrong, it is on you(17:7).

wa in asaʾtum fa-lahā

وَإِنْ أَسَأْتُمْ فَلَهَا

fa-lahā	*asaʾtum*	*in*	*wa*
lo (it is) for it	you did evil	if	and

3. Whoever is guided, it is only for himself that he is guided

mani-htadā fa-innamā yahtadī linafsihi

مَنِ اهْتَدَىٰ فَإِنَّمَا يَهْتَدِي لِنَفْسِهِۦ

linafsihi	*yahtadī*	*fa-innamā*	*ihtadā*	*man*
for himself	he is guided	truly	was guided	whoever

and whoever goes astray, it is only against his own self (17:15).

wa man ḍalla fa-innamā yaḍillu ^{c}alayha

وَمَنْ ضَلَّ فَإِنَّمَا يَضِلُّ عَلَيْهَا

^{c}alayhā	*yaḍillu*	*fa-innamā*	*ḍalla*	*man*	*wa*
against it	he goes astray	then truly	went astray	whoever	and

4. Whoever strives hard, he strives for himself (29:6).

man jāhada fa-innamā yujāhidu linafsihi

مَنْ جٰهَدَ فَإِنَّمَا يُجٰهِدُ لِنَفْسِهِ

linafsihi	*yujāhidu*	*fa-innamā*	*jāhada*	*man*
for himself	he strives	then truly	strove	whoever

5. Whoever purifies himself, in fact he purifies himself for himself (35:18).

man tazakkā fa-innamā yatazakkā linafsihi

مَنْ تَزَكّٰى فَإِنَّمَا يَتَزَكّٰى لِنَفْسِهِ

linafsihi	*yatazakkā*	*fa-innamā*	*tazakka*	*man*
for himself	he is purified	then truly	was purified	whoever

6. Whoever is thankful (to God) is thankful for his own self (31:17).

man yashkur fa-innamā yashkuru linafsihi

مَنْ يَّشْكُرْ فَإِنَّمَا يَشْكُرُ لِنَفْسِهِ

inafsihi	*yashkuru*	*fa-innamā*	*yashkur*	*man*
for himself	he gives thanks	then truly	gives thanks	whoever

Let's see what you have learned from

Section 3: Moral Behavior is Beneficial:

Identification:

1. Whoever does wrong ...
2. The good we do is for ...

Section 4: Piety and Fear of God

1. The best provision is piety (2:197).

khayraz-zādit-taqwā

خَيْرَ الزَّادِ التَّقْوٰى

at-taqwā	*az-zād*	*khayra*
(is) (the) piety	(of) provision	(the) best

2. Fear God and know that God

wattaqūl-lāha wa-^{c}lamu annal-lāha

وَاتَّقُوا اللّٰهَ وَاعْلَمُوٓا أَنَّ اللّٰهَ

Allāh	*anna*	*a-^{c}lamu*	*wa*	*Allāh*	*wattaqū*
God	that	know	and	God	and fear

is with the Godfearing (2:194).

ma^{c}al-muttaqīn

مَعَ الْمُتَّقِينَ

al-muttaqīn	*ma^c*
the Godfearing	(is) with

3. Truly God loves the Godfearing (9:4).

innal-lāha yuḥibbul-muttaqīn

إِنَّ اللّٰهَ يُحِبُّ الْمُتَّقِينَ

al-muttaqīn	*yuḥibbu*	*Allāh*	*inna*
the Godfearing	loves	God	truly

4. Truly the noblest of you in God's eyes is the most pious (49:13).

inna akramakum ^{c}indal-lāh atqākum

إِنَّ أَكْرَمَكُمْ عِنْدَ اللّٰهِ أَتْقٰكُمْ

atqākum	*Allāh*	*^{c}inda*	*akramkum*	*inna*
(is) the most pious of you	God	with	the noblest of you	truly

5. Aid one another in devoutness and piety (5:2).

taʿāwanū ʿalāl-birr wat-taqwā

تَعَاوَنُوا عَلَى الْبِرِّ وَالتَّقْوٰى

at-taqwā	*wa*	*al-birri*	*ʿalā*	*taʿāwanū*
(the) piety	and	(the) devoutness	on	aid one another

6. God delivers those who fear (Him)

yunajjīl-lāhul-ladhīnat-taqaw

وَيُنَجِّي اللّٰهُ الَّذِينَ اتَّقَوْا

ittaqaw	*al-ladhīna*	*Allāh*	*yunajjī*
who fear (Him)	those who	God	delivers

to their place of salvation; touches them not

bimafāzatihim lā yamassuhumu-s

بِمَفَازَتِهِمْ لَا يَمَسُّهُمُ

yamassuhum	*lā*	*bimafāzatihim*
touches them	not	to their place of salvation

evil and they shall not grieve (39:61).

-sūʾu wa lā hum yaḥzanūn

السُّوٓءُ وَلَا هُمْ يَحْزَنُونَ

yaḥzanūn	*humlā*	*wa*	*as-sūʾu*
grieve	they not	and	(the) evil

7. Whoever fears God, He will forgive him

may-yattaqil-lāha yukaffir ʿanhu

مَنْ يَتَّقِ اللّٰهَ يُكَفِّرْ عَنْهُ

ʿanhu	*yukaffir*	*Allāh*	*yattaqi*	*man*
(from) him	(He) forgives	God	fears	whoever

his misdeeds and enlarge his reward for him (65:5).

sayyiʾātihi wa yuᶜẓim lahu ajran

سَيِّـَٔاتِهِۦ وَيُعْظِمْ لَهُۥٓ أَجْرًا

ajran	*lahu*	*yuᶜẓim*	*wa*	*sayyiʾātihi*
(his) reward	for him	magnifies	and	his misdeeds

Let's see what you have learned from

Section 4: Piety and Fear of God:

Identification:

1. The best provision according to 2:197.
2. According to 2:194, who is with the Godfearing.

Clarification:

3. Explain who the noblest in God's eyes is.

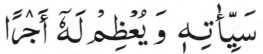

Section 5: Attitude Towards Parents

1. We have enjoined upon human beings kindness to parents (29:8).

waṣṣaynāl-insān biwālidayhi ḥusnan

وَصَّيْنَا ٱلْإِنسَٰنَ بِوَٰلِدَيْهِ إِحْسَٰنًا

ḥusnan	*biwālidayhi*	*al-insān*	*waṣṣaynā*
kindness	to his parents	(the) human being	We have enjoined

2. We have enjoined upon the human being beneficence to parents (46:15).

waṣṣaynāl-insān biwālidayhi iḥsānan

وَصَّيْنَا ٱلْإِنسَٰنَ بِوَٰلِدَيْهِ حُسْنًا

iḥsānan	*biwālidayhi*	*insān*	*waṣṣaynā*
beneficence	to his parents	(the) human being	We have enjoined

3. Accompany them in the world fittingly (31:15).

ṣāḥibhuma fīd-dunyā maᶜrūfan

صَاحِبْهُمَا فِي ٱلدُّنْيَا مَعْرُوفًا

maᶜrūfan	*ad-dunyā*	*fī*	*ṣāḥibhuma*
fittingly	the world	in	accompany them

4. Be kind to parents.

bil-wālidayn iḥsānan

بِٱلْوَٰلِدَيْنِ إِحْسَٰنًا ط

iḥsānan	*bil-wālidayn*
(be) kindly	to the parents

If either or both attain old age in your lifetime then do not

immā yablughanna ᶜindakal-kibara aḥaduhumā aw kilāhuma fa-lā

إِمَّا يَبْلُغَنَّ عِندَكَ ٱلْكِبَرَ أَحَدُهُمَآ أَوْ كِلَاهُمَا فَلَا

fa-lā kilāhuma	*aw aḥaduhumā*	*al-kibar*	*ᶜindaka*	*yablughanna*	*immā*
then both not	or one of them of them	(the) old age	with you	attains	if

say to them a word of displeasure and do not rebuff them and

taqul lahumā uffiw-wa lā tanhar humā wa

تَقُل لَّهُمَآ أُفٍّ وَّلَا تَنْهَرْهُمَا وَ

wa	*humā*	*tanhar*	*lā*	*wa*	*uff*	*lahumā*	*taqul*
and	them	rebuff	not	and	a word of displeasure	to them	say

speak to them with kindness

qul lahumā qawlan karīman

قُل لَّهُمَا قَوْلًا كَرِيمًا

karīman	*qawlan*	*lahumā*	*qul*
kindly	a word	to them	say

and lower to them the wing of the humility of mercy.

wa-khfiḍ lahumā janāḥadh-dhulli minar-raḥma

وَاخْفِضْ لَهُمَا جَنَاحَ الذُّلِّ مِنَ الرَّحْمَةِ

ar-raḥmattin min	*adh-dhulli*	*janāḥa*	*lahumā*	*ikhfiḍ*	*wa*
(the) mercy of	the humility	(the) wing (of)	to them	lower	and

Say, 'My Lord! Have mercy on them

wa qul rabbi-rḥamhumā

وَقُل رَّبِّ ارْحَمْهُمَا

irḥamhumā	*rabbi*	*qul*	*wa*
have mercy on them	my Lord	say	and

just as they brought me up when I was little' (17:23-24).

kamā rabbaynī ṣaghīran

كَمَا رَبَّيَانِي صَغِيرًا

ṣaghīran	*rabbaynī*	*kamā*
(when I was) little	they brought me up	just as

Let's see what you have learned from

Section 5: Attitude Towards Parents:

Identification:

1. Treatment of parents according to 17:23-24?
2. Prayer for one's parents (17:23-24)?

Clarification:

3. Why do we respect our parents?
4. What two things has God asked us to do towards our parents in 29:8 and 46:15?

Section 6: Courtesy and Human Relations

1. Show kindness to parents, relatives,

bilwālidayn iḥsānaw-wa dhīl-qurbā

بِالْوَٰلِدَيْنِ إِحْسَانًا وَذِي الْقُرْبَىٰ

dhīl-qurbā	*wa*	*iḥsānan*	*bilwālidayn*
(to the) kindred	and	(be) kindly	to the parents

the orphans and the destitute (2:83).

wal-yatāmā wal-masākīn

وَالْيَتَٰمَىٰ وَالْمَسَٰكِينِ

al-masākin	*wa*	*al-yatāmā*	*wa*
the destitute	and	the orphans	and

2. Whatever wealth you spend, let it be for parents,

mā anfaqtum min khayrin fa-lil-wālidayn

مَآ أَنفَقْتُم مِّنْ خَيْرٍ فَلِلْوَٰلِدَيْنِ

fa-lil-wālidayn	*khayrin*	*min*	*anfaqtum*	*mā*
then for the parents	good	of	you spent	what

relatives, orphans, the destitute,

wal-aqrabīn wal-yatāmā wal-masākīn

وَالْأَقْرَبِينَ وَالْيَتَٰمَىٰ وَالْمَسَٰكِينِ

al-masākīn	*wa*	*al-yatāmā*	*wa*	*al-aqrabīn*	*wa*
the destitute	and	the orphans	and	(the) relatives	and

and the wayfarer (2:215).

wa-bnis-sabīl

وَابْنِ السَّبِيلِ

as-sabīl	*ibn*	*wa*
(of) the road	(the) son	and

3. Be kindly to parents, kinsfolk,

bil-wālidayn iḥsānaw-wa bi-dhīl-qurbā

بِالْوَٰلِدَيْنِ إِحْسَٰنًا وَبِذِي الْقُرْبَىٰ

bi-dhīl-qurbā	*wa*	*iḥsānan*	*bil-wālidayn*
to kindred	and	(be) kindly	to the parents

orphans, the needy, the neighboring

wal-yatāmā wal-masākīn wal-jār

وَالْيَتَٰمَىٰ وَالْمَسَٰكِينِ وَالْجَارِ

al-jār	*wa*	*al-masākīn*	*wa*	*al-yatāmā*	*wa*
the neighbor	and	the destitute	and	the orphans	and

kinsman and the neighbor who is not of your kin,

dhīl-qurbā wal-jāril-junub

ذِي الْقُرْبَىٰ وَالْجَارِ الْجُنُبِ

al-junub	*al-jār*	*wa*	*dhīl-qurbā-*
(the) unrelated	the neighbor	and	kinsman

the companion, the wayfarer, and what your right hand possesses (4:36).

waṣ-ṣaḥib bil-jambi wa-bnis-sabīl wa mā malakatu aymānukum

وَالصَّاحِبِ بِالْجَنْبِ وَابْنِ السَّبِيلِ وَمَا مَلَكَتْ أَيْمَٰنُكُمْ

aymānukum	*malakat*	*mā*	*wa*	*as-sabil*	*ibn*	*wa*	*bil-jambi*	*aṣ-ṣaḥibi*	*wa*
your right hands possessed		that which	and	the wayfarer		and	at (the) side	the friend	and

4. Give the kinsmen, the needy, and the wayfarer their due (30:38).

fa-āti dhāl-qurbā ḥaqqahu wal-miskīn wa-bnas-sabīl

فَـَٔاتِ ذَا الْقُرْبَىٰ حَقَّهُۥ وَالْمِسْكِينَ وَابْنَ السَّبِيلِ

as-sabīl	*ibn*	*wa*	*al-miskīn*	*wa*	*ḥaqqahu*	*dhāl-qurbā*	*fa-āti*
the road	the wayfarer)	and	the destitute	and	his due	the relative	so give

5. Do not be harsh to the orphan (93:9).

fa-ammāl-yatīm fa-lā taqhar

فَأَمَّا الْيَتِيمَ فَلَا تَقْهَرْ

taqhar	*fa-lā*	*al-yatīm*	*fa-ammā*
be harsh	so not	the orphan	then as for

6. Do not chide the beggar (93:10).

ammās-sā°il fa-lā tanhar

أَمَّا السَّائِلَ فَلَا تَنْهَرْ

tanhar	*fa-lā*	*as-sā°il*	*ammā*
repulse (him)	then not	the beggar	as for

Let's find out what you have learned from

Section 6: Courtesy and Human Relations:

Identification:

1. Orphan (93:9)
2. Beggar (93:10)

Clarification:

3. List the nine people verse 4:36 tells us to be good to.
4. Explain who we should spend our wealth for according to 2:215.

Section 7: Why be good?

1. Do good! Truly God loves the doers of good (2:195).

aḥsinū innal-lāha yuḥibbu-l-muḥsinīn

أَحْسِنُوا إِنَّ اللّٰهَ يُحِبُّ الْمُحْسِنِينَ

al-muḥsinīn	*yuḥibbu*	*Allāh*	*inna*	*aḥsinū*
the doers of good	loves	God	truly	do good

2. Truly God is with the doers of good (29:69).

inna-llāha la-ma^{c}al-muḥsinīn

إِنَّ اللّٰهَ لَمَعَ الْمُحْسِنِينَ

al-muḥsinīn	*la-ma^{c}a*	*Allāh*	*inna*
the doers of good	(is) indeed with	God	truly

3. Truly God is with those who fear Him

innal-lāha ma^{c}al-ladhīnat-taqaw

إِنَّ اللّٰهَ مَعَ الَّذِينَ اتَّقَوا

ittaqaw	*al-ladhīna*	*ma^{c}a*	*Allāh*	*inna*
fear (Him)	those who	(is) with	God	truly

and those who do good (16:128).

wal-ladhīna hum muḥsinūn

وَّالَّذِينَ هُم مُّحْسِنُونَ

muḥsinūn	*hum*	*al-ladhīna*	*wa*
doers of good	they (are)	those who	and

4. Truly God commands justice and goodness (16:90).

innal-lāha ya^{ɔ}muru bil-^{c}adl wal-iḥsān

إِنَّ اللّٰهَ يَأْمُرُ بِالْعَدْلِ وَالْإِحْسٰنِ

al-iḥsān	*wa*	*bil-^{c}adl*	*ya^{ɔ}muru*	*Allāha*	*inna*
(the) charity	and	(with) justice	commands	God	truly

5. Whoever earns any good, We shall increase

may-yaqtarifu ḥasanatan nazidu

مَن يَقْتَرِفْ حَسَنَةً نَّزِدْ

nazid	*ḥasanatan*	*yaqtarif*	*man*
We increase	good	earns	whoever

goodness in respect thereof (42:23).

lahu fīhā ḥusnan

لَهُۥ فِيهَا حُسْنًا

ḥusnan	*fīhā*	*lahu*
goodness	in it	for him

6. For those who did good in this world there is good (39:10).

lil-adhīna aḥsanū fī hādhihi-d-dunyā ḥasanatun

لِلَّذِينَ أَحْسَنُوا۟ فِى هَٰذِهِ ٱلدُّنْيَا حَسَنَةٌ

ḥasanatun	*ad-dunyā*	*hādhihi*	*fī*	*aḥsanū*	*lil-adhīna*
(is) good	(the) world	this	in	did good	for those who

7. Truly God has prepared for women doing good

innal-lāha aʿadda lilmuḥsināt

إِنَّ ٱللَّهَ أَعَدَّ لِلْمُحْسِنَٰتِ

lil-muḥsināt	*aʿadda*	*Allah*	*inna*
for women doing good	has prepared	God	truly

a great reward amongst you (33:29).

minkunna ajran ʿaẓīman

مِنكُنَّ أَجْرًا عَظِيمًا

ʿaẓīman	*ajran*	*minkunna*
great	a reward	among you (women)

8. *Truly the good deeds remove the misdeeds (11:114).*

innal-ḥasanat yudhhibnas-sayyiāt

إِنَّ الْحَسَنٰتِ يُذْهِبْنَ السَّيِّأٰتِ

as-sayyiāt	*yudhhibna*	*al-ḥasanat*	*inna*
the misdeeds	remove	the good deeds	truly

9. *Truly God does not waste the reward of the doers of good (9:120).*

inna-llāha lā yuḍīᶜu ajrat-l-muḥsinīn

إِنَّ اللّٰهَ لَا يُضِيعُ أَجْرَ الْمُحْسِنِينَ

al-muḥsinīn	*ajra*	*yuḍīᶜu*	*lā*	*Allāha*	*inna*
(of) the doers of good	(the) reward	waste	not	God	truly

Let's find out what you have learned from

Section 7: Why be good?

Identification:

1. Who does God loves?
2. With whom is God?

Clarification:

3. Explain what God commands in 16:90.
4. Explain what positive traits eliminate according to 11:114.

Section 8: Charms of Everyday Conversation

1. Speak nicely to people (2:83).

qūlū lin-nās ḥusnan

قُولُوا لِلنَّاسِ حُسْنًا

ḥusnan	*lin-nās*	*qūlū*
nicely	to (the) people	speak

2. Speak the right speech (33:70).

qūlū qawlan sadīdan

قُولُوا قَوْلًا سَدِيدًا

sadīdan	*qawlan*	*qūlū*
right	a word	say

3. Say to them a friendly word (4:5).

qūlū lahum qawlam-ma^{c}rūfan

قُولُوا لَهُمْ قَوْلًا مَّعْرُوفًا

ma^{c}rūfan	*qawlam*	*lahum*	*qūlū*
friendly	a word	to them	say

4. Lower your voice. Truly

wa-ghḍuḍ min ṣawtika inna

وَاغْضُضْ مِن صَوْتِكَ إِنَّ

inna	*ṣawtika*	*min*	*aghḍuḍ*	*wa*
truly	your voice	(from)	lower	and

the most repugnant of voices is the voice of the ass (31:19).

ankaral-aṣwāt laṣawtul-ḥamīr

أَنكَرَ الْأَصْوَاتِ لَصَوْتُ الْحَمِيرِ

al-ḥamīr	*la-ṣawtu*	*al-aṣwāt*	*ankar*
the ass	(is) (the) voice (of)	(the) voices	most repugnant (of)

5. *A friendly word and forgiveness are better*

qawlun ma^c^rūfuw-wa maghfiratun khayru-

قَوْلٌ مَّعْرُوفٌ وَمَغْفِرَةٌ خَيْرٌ

khayrun	*maghfiratun*	*wa*	*ma^c^rūfn*	*qawlun*
(are) better	forgiveness	and	friendly	a word

than charity followed by injury (2:263).

m-min ṣadaqatiy-yatba^c^hā adhan

مِّن صَدَقَةٍ يَتْبَعُهَآ أَذًى

adhan	*yatba^c^hā*	*ṣadaqatin*	*min*
injury	follows it	charity	than

6. *When you are greeted with a greeting, then answer*

idhā ḥuyyītum bitaḥīyatin fa-ḥayyū

إِذَا حُيِّيتُم بِتَحِيَّةٍ فَحَيُّوا

fa-ḥayyū	*bitaḥīyatin*	*ḥuyyītum*	*idhā*
then answer	with a greeting	you are greeted	when

back with one better, or (at least) return the same (4:86).

bi aḥsana minhā aw ruddūhā

بِأَحْسَنَ مِنْهَآ أَوْ رُدُّوهَا

ruddūhā	*aw*	*minhā*	*bi-aḥsana*
return it	or	than it	with better

7. *Who is better in speech than the one*

man aḥsanu qawlam-miman

مَنْ أَحْسَنُ قَوْلًا مِّمَّن

mimman	*qawlan*	*aḥsanu*	*man*
than he who	in speech	(is) better	who

who summons (people) unto God, and performed

da^{c}ā ilāl-lāhi wa ^{c}amila

دَعَآ إِلَى اللهِ وَعَمِلَ

^{c}amila	*wa*	*Allāh*	*ilā*	*da^{c}ā*
performed	and	God	to	called

a good deed and says, 'Truly I am

ṣāliḥan-wa qāla innanī

صَٰلِحًا وَّقَالَ إِنَّنِي

innanī	*qāla*	*wa*	*ṣāliḥan*
truly I am	said	and	a good deed

of the believers' (41:33).

minal-muslimīn

مِنَ الْمُسْلِمِينَ

al-muslimīn	*min*
the believers	of

Let's find out what you have learned from

Section 8: Charms of Everyday Conversation:

Identification:

1. The harshest of sounds (31:19).

Clarification:

2. What kind of speech is the best kind according to 41:33?
3. Explain what is better than charity followed by injury (2:263).

Section 9: The Value of Truth

1. Whosoever comes with the Truth and

al-ladhī jāʾa biṣ-ṣidqi wa

اَلَّذِيْ جَآءَ بِالصِّدْقِ وَ

wa	biṣ-ṣidq	jāʾa	al-ladhī
and	with the Truth	came	he who

believes in it; they are the devout (39:33).

ṣaddaqa bihī ūlāʾika humul-muttaqūn

صَدَّقَ بِهٖ أُولَٰٓئِكَ هُمُ الْمُتَّقُوْنَ

al-muttaqūn	hum	ūlāʾika	bihī	ṣaddaqa
the devout	they (are)	those	in it	believed

2. Be with the truthful (9:119).

kūnū maʿaṣ-ṣādiqīn

كُوْنُوْا مَعَ الصّٰدِقِيْنَ

aṣ-ṣādiqīn	maʿa	kūnū
the truthful	with	be

3. Truly the false will vanish (17:81).

innal-bāṭila kāna zahūqan

إِنَّ الْبَاطِلَ كَانَ زَهُوْقًا

zahūqan	kāna	al-bāṭila	inna
vanishing	was	the false	truly

4. Cover not the truth with the false

lā talbisūl-haqqā bil-bāṭil wa

لَا تَلْبِسُوا الْحَقَّ بِالْبَاطِلِ وَ

bil-bāṭil	al-haqqā	talbisūl	lā
with the false	the truth	cover	not

nor conceal the truth while you know it (2:42).

taktumūl-haqqā wa antum ta^{c}lamūn

تَكْتُمُوا الْحَقَّ وَأَنْتُمْ تَعْلَمُونَ

ta^{c}lamūn	*antum*	*wa*	*al-haqqā*	*taktumū*
know	you	and	the truth	conceal

5. Oh those who believe! Why do you say

yā ayyuhāl ladhīna āmanū lima taqūlūn

يَا أَيُّهَا الَّذِينَ آمَنُوا لِمَ تَقُولُونَ

taqūlūn	*lima*	*āmanū*	*al-ladhīna*	*yā ayyuhā*
you say	why	believed	who	O you

that which you do not do (61:2)?

mā lā taf^{c}alūn

مَا لَا تَفْعَلُونَ

taf^{c}alūn	*lā*	*mā*
you do	not	what

Let's find out what you have learned from

Section 9: The Value of Truth:

Identification:

1. Pious (39:33)
2. Falsehood (17:81)

Clarification:

3. Give an example from your own life where you concealed the truth and explain what happened.
4. What are some things you say but do not do?

Section10: Keep Your Promises!

1. O you who believe! Keep your promises (5:1).

yā ayyuhāl-ladhīna āmanū awfū bil^{c}uqūdi

يَاأَيُّهَا الَّذِينَ آمَنُوٓا أَوْفُوا بِالْعُقُودِ

bil^{c}uqūdi	*awfū*	*āmanū*	*ladhīna*	*yā ayyuhā*
(with) the agreements	fulfill	believed	who	O you

2. He who keeps his promise and fears (God):

man awfā bi^{c}ahdihi wa-ttaqā

مَنْ أَوْفَىٰ بِعَهْدِهِ وَاتَّقَىٰ

ittaqā	*wa*	*bi-^{c}ahdihi*	*awfā*	*man*
feared God	and	(with) his covenant	fulfilled	he

truly God loves the devout (3:76).

fa inna-llāha yuḥibbul-muttaqīn

فَإِنَّ اللَّهَ يُحِبُّ الْمُتَّقِينَ

muttaqīn	*yuḥibbu*	*Allāh*	*fa-inna*
the devout	loves	God	for truly

3. Fulfill the covenant. Truly the covenant will be questioned (17:34).

awfū bil-^{c}ahdi-inna ^{c}ahda kāna mas$^{\supset}$ūlan

أَوْفُوا بِالْعَهْدِ إِنَّ الْعَهْدَ كَانَ مَسْئُولًا

mas$^{\supset}$ūlan	*kāna*	*^{c}ahda*	*inna*	*bil-^{c}ahdi*	*awfū*
asked about	would be	the covenant	truly	(with) the covenant	fulfill

Let's find out what you have learned from

Section 10: Keep Your Promises!:

Identification:

1. The faithful should have?

Fill in the Blanks:

2. Fulfill the ___________ (17:34).

Clarification:

3. According to 3:76, God loves those who keep their promises and?

Section 11: Patience and Perseverance

1. Oh you believe! Be patient and console (3:200).

yā ayyuhāl-ladhīna āmanū-ṣbirū wa sābirū

يَٰأَيُّهَا الَّذِينَ أَمَنُوا اصْبِرُوا وَ صَابِرُوا

sābirū	*wa*	*iṣbirū*	*āmanū*	*al-ladhīna*	*yā ayyuhā*
console	and	be patient	believed	who	O you

2. God loves the patient (3:146).

allāhu yuḥibbuṣ-ṣābirīn

اللهُ يُحِبُّ الصَّٰبِرِينَ

aṣ-ṣābirīn	*yuḥibbu*	*Allāh*
the patient	loves	God

3. Truly God is with the patient (8:46).

inna-llāha ma^{c}aṣ-ṣābirīn

إِنَّ اللهَ مَعَ الصَّٰبِرِينَ

aṣ-ṣābirīn	*ma^{c}a*	*Allāh*	*inna*
the patient	with	God (is)	truly

4. So be patient with a beautiful patience (70:5).

fa-ṣbir ṣabran jamīlan

فَاصْبِرْ صَبْرًا جَمِيلًا

jamīlan	*ṣabran*	*fa-ṣbir*
beautiful	a patience	so be patient

5. Be patient even as among the Messengers were the patient (46:35)

fa-ṣbir kamā ṣabara ūlūl-^{c}azm minar-rusul

فَاصْبِرْ كَمَا صَبَرَ أُولُوا الْعَزْمِ مِنَ الرُّسُلِ

ar-rusul	*min*	*al-^{c}azm*	*ūlū*	*ṣabara*	*kamā*	*fa-ṣbir*
the Messengers	from among	(the) determination	(the) possessors (of)	were patient	even as	so be patient

6. Bear patiently that which afflicts you. Truly

wa-ṣbir ᶜalā mā aṣābaka inna

وَاصْبِرْ عَلَىٰ مَآ أَصَابَكَ ۖ إِنَّ

inna	*aṣābaka*	*mā*	*ᶜalā*	*wa-ṣbir*
truly	afflicted you	that which	(on)	and bear patiently

that is the firmness of affairs (31:17).

dhālika min ᶜazmil-umūr

ذَٰلِكَ مِنْ عَزْمِ الْأُمُورِ

al-umūr	*ᶜazmi*	*min*	*dhālika*
(the) affairs	the firmness (of)	of	that (is)

7. Seek help in patience and prayer (2:153).

istaᶜīnū biṣ-ṣabr waṣ-ṣālati

اسْتَعِينُوا بِالصَّبْرِ وَالصَّلَوٰةِ

aṣ-ṣalāti	*wa*	*biṣ-ṣabr*	*istaᶜīnū*
(the) prayer	and	with (the) patience	seek help

8. We shall indeed reward those who are patient

la-najziyannal-ladhīna ṣabarū

لَنَجْزِيَنَّ الَّذِينَ صَبَرُوٓا

ṣabarū	*al-ladhīna*	*la-najziyanna*
were patient	those who	We shall indeed reward

with a reward for the best (of) their deeds (16:96).

ajrahum bi-aḥsani mā kānū yaᶜmalūn

أَجْرَهُم بِأَحْسَنِ مَا كَانُوا يَعْمَلُونَ

yaᶜmalūn	*mā*	*bi-aḥsani*	*ajrahum*
they were doing	that which	with the best (of)	their reward

Let's find out what you have learned from

Section 11: Patience and Perseverance:

Identification:

1. The faithful should have?
2. Seek help in (2:153).

Clarification:

3. Explain a situation in your life that you had to bear patiently.
4. Who does God love in 3:146.

Section 12: The Harvest of Hard Work

1. A human being can have nothing but what he strives for (53:39).

laysa lil-insān illā mā saʿā

لَّيْسَ لِلْإِنسَٰنِ إِلَّا مَا سَعَىٰ

saʿā	*mā*	*illā*	*lil-insān*	*laysa*
he strove for	that which	except	for the human being	there is not

2. Whoever performs good deeds

fa-may-yaʿmal minaṣ-ṣāliḥāt wa

فَمَن يَعْمَلْ مِنَ ٱلصَّٰلِحَٰتِ وَ

wa	*aṣ-ṣāliḥāt*	*min*	*yaʿmal*	*fa-man*
and	(the) good deeds	of	performs	for he who

and is a believer: his efforts will not be rejected (21:94).

huwa muʾmin fa-lā kufrān lisaʿyihi

هُوَ مُؤْمِنٌ فَلَا كُفْرَانَ لِسَعْيِهِۦ

lisaʿyihi	*kufrān*	*fa-lā*	*muʾmin*	*huwa*
for his effort	rejection	then not	a believer	he (is)

Let's find out what you have learned from

Section 12: The Harvest of Hard Work:

Fill in the blanks:

1. A human being has ________ (52:29)?
2. Whoever performs good deeds and is a believer ______ (21:94).

Section 13: Good Table Manners

1. Eat of the good things which We have provided you (2:172).

kulū min ṭayyibāt mā razaqnākum

كُلُوا مِن طَيِّبَٰتِ مَا رَزَقْنَٰكُمْ

razaqnākum	*mā*	*ṭayyibāt*	*min*	*kulū*
We have provided you	which	good things	out of	eat

2. Eat whatever is lawful and good on the earth (2:168).

kulū mimmā fil-ᶜarḍ ḥalālan ṭayyiban

كُلُوا مِمَّا فِي الْأَرْضِ حَلَٰلًا طَيِّبًا

ṭayyiban	*ḥalālan*	*al-ᶜarḍ*	*fī*	*mimmā*	*kulū*
good	lawful	the earth	on	whatever (is)	eat

3. Eat not those (meats) over which God's Name has not been pronounced (6:118).

kulū mimmā dhukira-smul-lāhi ᶜalayhi

فَكُلُوا مِمَّا ذُكِرَ اسْمُ اللَّهِ عَلَيْهِ

ᶜalayhi	*Allāh*	*ismu*	*dhukira*	*mimmā*	*kulū*
on it	(of) God	(the) name	pronounced	that which	eat

4. Do not eat (meat) if the Name has not been pronounced;

lā taᵓkulū mimmā lam yudhkira-smu-

لَا تَأْكُلُوا مِمَّا لَمْ يُذْكَرِ اسْمُ

ismu	*yudhkira*	*lam*	*mimmā*	*taᵓkulū*	*lā*
Name	pronounced	not	which	eat	not

that is truly sinfulness (6:121).

-llāhi ᶜalayhi wa innahu la-fisq

اللَّهِ عَلَيْهِ وَإِنَّهُ لَفِسْقٌ

la-fisq	*innahu*	*wa*	*ᶜalayhi*	*Allāh*
indeed sinfulness	truly it (is)	and	on it	(of) God

5. There is no sin for you whether you eat

laysa ᶜalaykum junāḥ an taᵓkulū

لَيْسَ عَلَيْكُمْ جُنَاحٌ أَنْ تَأْكُلُوا

taᵓkulū	*an*	*junāḥ*	*ᶜalaykum*	*laysa*
eat	to	a sin	on you	there is not

together or separately (24:61).

jamīᶜan aw ashtātan

جَمِيعًا أَوْ أَشْتَاتًا

ashtātan	*aw*	*jamīᶜan*
separately	or	together

6. Eat and drink but do not be immoderate (7:31).

kulū wa-shrabū wa lā tusrifū

كُلُوا وَاشْرَبُوا وَلَا تُسْرِفُوا

tusrifū	*lā*	*wa*	*ishrabū*	*wa*	*kulū*
be immoderate	not	and	drink	and	eat

7. Truly He has forbidden you carrion,

innamā ḥarrama ᶜalaykumul-maytata

إِنَّمَا حَرَّمَ عَلَيْكُمُ الْمَيْتَةَ

al-maytata	*ᶜalaykum*	*ḥarrama*	*innamā*
(the) carrion	on you(He)	has forbidden	truly

blood, the meat of the pig, and

wad-dam wa laḥmal-khinzīr wa

وَالدَّمَ وَلَحْمَ الْخِنْزِيرِ وَ

wa	*al-khinzir*	*laḥma*	*wa*	*ad-dam*	*wa*
and	(of) the pig	(the) meat	and	(the) blood	and

that which has been offered up to other than God (16:115).

mā uhilla lighayril-lāhi bihi

مَآ أُهِلَّ لِغَيۡرِ ٱللَّهِ بِهِۦ

Allāh	*li-ghayri*	*uhilla*	*mā*
God	to other (than)	has been offered up	that which

Let's find out what you have learned from

Section 13: Good Table Manners:

Identification:

1. Pork
2. Dead meat

Clarification:

3. Explain what meat is lawful to eat based on 16:115.

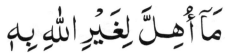

Section 14: Personal Health and Hygiene

1. Purify your clothes (74:4).

thiyābaka fa-ṭahhir

وَثِيَابَكَ فَطَهِّرْ

fa-ṭahhir	*thiyābaka*
(then) purify it	your clothing

2. Shun pollution (74:5).

ar-rujuz fa-hjur

وَالرُّجْزَ فَاهْجُرْ

fa-hjur	*ar-rujuz*
(then) shun	(the) pollution

Let's find out what you have learned from

Section 14: Personal Health and Hygiene:

Fill in the blanks:

1. Impurity ______________ (74:5).
2. Purify ______________ (74:4).

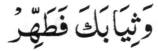

Section 15: Forgiveness and Forbearance

1. Forgive and pardon (2:109).

fa^{c}fū wa-ṣfaḥū

فَاعْفُوا وَاصْفَحُوا

iṣfaḥū	*wa*	*fa^{c}fū*
pardon	and	so forgive

2. Overlook with a gracious forgiveness (15:85).

fa-ṣfaḥiṣ-ṣafḥal-jamīl

فَاصْفَحِ الصَّفْحَ الْجَمِيلَ

al-jamīl	*aṣ-ṣafḥ*	*fa-ṣfaḥ*
(the) beautiful	(the) forgiveness	so forgive

3. Whosoever was patient and forgave: that truly is

man ṣabara wa ghafara inna dhālika

مَنْ صَبَرَ وَغَفَرَ إِنَّ ذٰلِكَ

dhālika	*inna*	*ghafara*	*wa*	*ṣabara*	*man*
that	truly	forgave	and	was patient	whoever

of the firmness of affairs (42:43).

la-min ^{c}azmil-umūr

لَمِنْ عَزْمِ الْأُمُورِ

al-umūr	*^{c}azmi*	*la-min*
(the) affairs	(the) firmness (of)	(is) indeed of

4. If you forgive that is nearest to piety (2:237).

an ta^{c}fū aqrab lit-taqwā

أَنْ تَعْفُوا أَقْرَبُ لِلتَّقْوٰى

lit-taqwā	*aqrab*	*ta^{c}fū*	*an*
to (the) piety	(is) nearer	forgive	to

Let's see what you have learned from

Section 15: Forgiveness and Forebearance:

Clarification:

1. What is nearest piety (2:237)?
2. What is the firmness of affairs (42:43)?
3. Have you been able to forgive those who have hurt you?

Section 16: Friendship and Co-operation

1. Truly the believers are brethren so make peace

innamāl-muʾminūn ikhwatun fa-ṣliḥū

إِنَّمَا الْمُؤْمِنُونَ إِخْوَةٌ فَأَصْلِحُوا

fa-ṣliḥū	*ikhwatun*	*al-muʾminūn*	*innamā*
so make peace	brethren	the believers (are)	truly

between your brothers (49:10).

bayna akhawaykum

بَيْنَ أَخَوَيْكُمْ

akhawaykum	*bayna*
your brothers	between

2. The believing men and the believing women, some of them

wal-muʾminūn wal-muʾmināt baʿḍuhum

وَالْمُؤْمِنُونَ وَالْمُؤْمِنَٰتُ بَعْضُهُمْ

baʿḍuhum	*al-muʾmināt*	*wa*	*al-muʾminūn*	*wa*
some of them	the female believers (are)	and	the male believers	and

are friends to one another (9:71)

awliyā baʿḍin

أَوْلِيَآءُ بَعْضٍ

baʿḍin	*awliyā*
(of) some	friends

3. Do not forget grace among yourselves (2:237).

lā tansawl-faḍla baynakum

لَا تَنْسَوُا الْفَضْلَ بَيْنَكُمْ

baynakumal-faḍla	*tansaw*	*lā*
among you(the) grace	forget	not

4. Repel (evil) with what is better; then he,

idfa^c bil-latī hiya aḥsan fa-idhā

إِدْفَعْ بِالَّتِي هِيَ أَحْسَنُ فَإِذَا

fa-idhā	*aḥsan*	*hiya*	*bil-latī*	*idfa^c*
for then	better	it (is)	with that which	repulse

between whom there was

-l-ladhī baynaka wa baynahu

الَّذِي بَيْنَكَ وَبَيْنَهُ

baynahu	*wa*	*baynaka*	*al-ladhī*
(between) him	and	between you	he who

enmity, he will become as though he was a good friend (41:34).

^{c}adāwatun ka-annahu walīyun ḥamīm

عَدَاوَةٌ كَأَنَّهُ وَلِيٌّ حَمِيمٌ

ḥamīm	*walīyun*	*ka-annahu*	*^{c}adāwatun*
warm	a friend	he will be as though	(is) enmity

5. Hold fast to God's rope all together and be not dispersed (3:103).

wa^c-taṣimū biḥablil-lāhi jamī^{c}an wa lā tafarraqū

وَاعْتَصِمُوا بِحَبْلِ اللَّهِ جَمِيعًا وَلَا تَفَرَّقُوا

tafarraqū	*lā*	*wa*	*jamī^{c}an*	*Allāh*	*bi-ḥabli*	*i^{c}taṣimū*	*wa*
disperse	not	and	all together	God	to the rope	hold fast	and

Let's find out what you have learned from
Section 16: Friendship and Co-operation:

Identification:

1. Believers (49:10)
2. Friends (9:71)

Clarification:

3. Explain an instance in your life where you would hold fast to God's rope and be not divided if you could.

Section 17: Islamic Social Etiquette

1. Do not enter houses other than

lā tadkhulū buyūtan ghayra

لَا تَدْخُلُوا بُيُوتًا غَيْرَ

ghayra	*buyūtan*	*tadkhulū*	*lā*
other than	houses	enter	not

your own until you have asked permission

buyūtikum hattā tastānisū

بُيُوتِكُمْ حَتَّىٰ تَسْتَأْنِسُوا

tastānisū	*hattā*	*buyūtikum*
you ask permission	until	your houses

and greeted their inmates (24:27).

wa tusallimū ^{c}alā ahlihā

وَتُسَلِّمُوا عَلَىٰٓ أَهْلِهَا

ahlihā	*^{c}alā*	*tusallimū*	*wa*
their folk	(on)	you greet	and

2. When you enter houses, greet

fa-idhā dakhaltum buyūtan fa-sallimū

فَإِذَا دَخَلْتُمْ بُيُوتًا فَسَلِّمُوا

fa-sallimū	*buyūtan*	*dakhaltum*	*fa-idhā*
then greet	houses	you entered	so when

each other with a greeting as from God,

^{c}alā anfusikum taḥīyatan min ^{c}indil-lāhi

عَلَىٰٓ أَنْفُسِكُمْ تَحِيَّةً مِّنْ عِنْدِ اللَّهِ

Allāh	*^{c}indi*	*min*	*taḥīyatan*	*anfusikum*	*^{c}alā*
God	(at)	from	a greeting	yourselves	(on)

a blessed good (24:61).

mubārakatan ṭayyibatan

مُبَٰرَكَةً طَيِّبَةً

ṭayyibatan	*mubārakatan*
good	blessed (and)

3. Do not say to one who extends to you a greeting,

lā taqūlū liman alqā ilaykumu

لَا تَقُولُوا لِمَنْ أَلْقَىٰٓ إِلَيْكُمُ

ilaykum	*alqā*	*liman*	*taqūlū*	*lā*
to you	extended	to one who	say	not

'You are not a believer' (4:94).

-s-salām lasta mu'minan

ٱلسَّلَٰمَ لَسْتَ مُؤْمِنًا

mu'minan	*lasta*	*as-salām*
believer	you are not	the salutation

4. When it was said to you to make room in

idhā qīla lakum tafassaḥū fī

إِذَا قِيلَ لَكُمْ تَفَسَّحُوا فِي

fī	*tafassaḥū*	*lakum*	*qīla*	*idhā*
in	make room	to you	it was said	when

assemblies, make room. God will make room

-l-majālis fa-fsaḥū yafsaḥil-lāhu

ٱلْمَجَٰلِسِ فَٱفْسَحُوا يَفْسَحِ ٱللَّهُ

Allāh	*yafsaḥ*	*fa-fsaḥū*	*al-majālis*
God	will make room	then make room	the assemblies

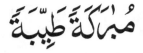

for you. When it is said, 'Rise up,' rise up (58:11).

lakum wa idhā qīla-nshuzū fa-nshuzū

لَكُمْ ج وَإِذَا قِيلَ انْشُزُوا فَانْشُزُوا

fa-nshuzū	*unshuzū*	*qīla*	*idhā*	*wa*	*lakum*
then rise up	rise up	it is said	when	and	for you

Let's find out what you have learned from

Section 17: Islamic Social Etiquette:

Identification:

1. Permission (24:27)
2. Peace (24:61)

Clarification:

3. What does 4:94 tell us not to say to one who greets us?

Section 18: Conclusion

These verses are just a small sample of the verses in the Quran dealing with the fruits of moral behavior. When we are guided by the Quran, we learn that God rewards our good deeds and that moral behavior is beneficial to us in this world and the next. We try to practice guarding against wrongdoing which is the only sign of superiority in Islam. We respect our parents and care for them in their old age. We are courteous towards others so they will be drawn to us as model human beings. God asks us to be good so He can reward us. We do not raise our voices so that we sound like braying asses which is the worst of sounds. God has told us in the Quran about the value of truth and keeping our promises, of showing patience and perseverance in every situation. God will reward our hard work for His path but we also need to learn good eating habits and have good personal hygiene so others will not turn away from us. We need to learn forgiveness and forbearance while developing friendships through cooperation with others. Finally, we are taught etiquette in the Quran, one form of which is not to enter anyone's home without his or her permission, to greet each other with a greeting of blessings and not to judge others who offer us such a greeting. God is the only judge.

Section Answers:

Section 1: Introduction

1. character building positive traits.
2. forgiving people.
3. Choose any three.
4. It means to see all of humanity as a unified nation of brotherhood/sisterhood.

Section 2: Reward for Good Deeds

1. Whoever believes in God and does good deeds.
2. Believe, do good and counsel each other to truth and patience.
3. God.
4. Those who believe in God and do good deeds.

Section 3: Moral Behavior is Beneficial

1. Is (acting) against his (her) own interests.
2. Ourselves.

Section 4: Piety and Fear of God

1. Piety.
2. God.
3. The most pious.

Section 5: Attitude Towards Parents

1. Without contempt or rebelling. Address them in respectful ways.
2. My Lord have mercy...
3. Because they brought us up when we were young and helpless.
4. Treat them with kindness and affection.

Section 6: Courtesy and Human Relations

1. The Quran tells us not to deal with them harshly.
2. Do not turn them away.
3. Parents, relatives, orphans, the needy, the near neighbor, the far neighbor, companions, the wayfarer and what our right hand possesses.
4. Parents, relatives, orphans, the needy and the traveler.

Section 7: Why be good?

1. God loves those who do good.
2. The right doers.
3. Justice and goodness.
4. Negative traits like envy, jealousy, inappropriate anger and so forth.

Section 8: Charms of Everyday Conversation

1. The braying of an ass.
2. Speech that summons others to God.
3. Kind words and forgiveness.

Section 9: The Value of Truth

1. Those who bring the truth and confirm it.
2. Even perishing.
3. Each response differs.
4. Each response differs.

Section 10: Keep Your Promises!

1. Keep your promises.
2. Covenant.
3. Guard against wrongdoing.

Section 11: Patience and Perseverance

1. Patience and perseverance.
2. In patience and prescribed prayer.
3. Each response differs.
4. The patient.

Section 12: The Harvest of Hard Work

1. ... nothing but what he (she) strives for.
2. ... his efforts will not be rejected.

Section 13: Good Table Manners

1. Forbidden to Muslims (7:31).
2. Forbidden to Muslims (7:31)
3. Each response differs.

Section 14: Personal Health and Hygiene

1. Avoid it.
2. your clothes (74:4).

Section 15: Forgiveness and Forbearance

1. To forgive.
2. To be patient and forgive.
3. Each response differs.

Section 16: Friendship and Co-operation

1. Are a single brotherhood.
2. Believing men and believing women.
3. Each response differs.

Section 17: Islamic Social Etiquette

1. Do not enter someone's house without permission.
2. When you enter, greet each other with a greeting of blessings.
3. Verse 4:94 tells us, "*Do not ...*"

5

Negative Traits to be Avoided

Section 1: Introduction

What is wrongdoing? How do we avoid the path of wrongdoing? This chapter offers some such simple verses from the Quran as add to our knowledge of actions which displease God. Each one of us faces various situations in our life. We often make right and wrong choices in our everyday affairs. These verses prove helpful in understanding the nature of wrongdoing. They enable us to avoid manifesting negative traits in our daily dealings.

Section 2: Avoiding the Negative

If you really intend to become a good citizen, always avoid wrongdoing. A wrongdoer never gains. His or her efforts end in failure and pain.

Section 3: Misdeeds Bring Pain

Our misdeeds bring pain to ourselves.

Section 4: Lying, Backbiting, Ridiculing Others

A good child should never lie. Backbiting and ridiculing others are undesirable acts.

Section 5: Boasting, Arrogance and Showing Off

Islam forbids boasting and showing off in any form.

Section 6: Mischief-Making

Mischievous activities are injurious to everyone.

Section 7: Oppression

We must avoid oppression, cruelty and all types of violence.

Section 8: Cheating and Stealing

Fraud and theft are unlawful deeds. Such bad acts require proper handling.

Section 9: Extravagance and Squandering

Why waste money? Such undesirable tendencies must be avoided.

Section 10: Misappropriation and Embezzlement

These are negative actions on our part.

Section 11: Mischievous Thoughts

Wrong thoughts must also be kept under proper control. Restraining these thoughts is essential for the wholesome growth of our character and personality.

Section 12: Misleading Friends

Friends who mislead us away from the Straight Path are dangerous. They must be avoided by all those who desire to be successful in both this life and the next.

Section 13: Conclusion

Section 2: Avoiding the Negative

1. He has made hateful to you unbelief, wickedness and rebellion (against God) (49:7).

karraha ilayhumul-kufr wal-fusūq wal-^{c}iṣyān

كَرَّهَ إِلَيْكُمُ الْكُفْرَ وَالْفُسُوقَ وَالْعِصْيَانَ

al-^{c}iṣyān *wa*	*al-fusūq*	*wa*	*al-kufr*	*ilayhum*	*karraha*
rebellion and	wickedness	and	unbelief	to you	He has made hateful

2. Satan threatens you with poverty and

ash-shayṭān ya^{c}idukumul-faqr wa

أَلشَّيْطٰنُ يَعِدُكُمُ الْفَقْرَ وَ

wa	*al-faqr*	*ya^{c}idukum*	*ash-shayṭān*
and	(with) poverty	threatens you	(the) satan

commands you to indecency (2:268).

ya^{c}murukum bil-faḥshā

يَأْمُرُكُم بِالْفَحْشَاءِ

bil-faḥshā	*ya^{c}murukum*
to (the) indecency	commands you

3. Do not follow the footsteps of satan.

lā tattaba^{c}ū khuṭuwātish-shayṭān

لَا تَتَّبِعُوا خُطُوٰتِ الشَّيْطٰنِ

ash-shayṭān	*khuṭuwāti*	*tattaba^{c}ū*	*lā*
satan	(the) footsteps (of)	follow do	not

Truly he is a clear enemy to you (2:168).

innahu lakum ^{c}udūwum-mubīn

إِنَّهُ لَكُمْ عَدُوٌّ مُّبِينٌ

mubīn	*^{c}udūwum*	*lakum*	*innahu*
clear	enemy	for you	truly (he is)

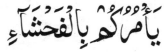

4. *Do not cooperate with each other in sin and hostility (5:2).*

lā taʿāwanū al-ʿālāl-ithm wal-ʿudwān

لَا تَعَاوَنُوا عَلَى الْإِثْمِ وَالْعُدْوَانِ

al-ʿudwān	*wa*	*al-ithm*	*ʿālā*	*taʿāwanū*	*lā*
(the) hostility	and	(the) sin	on	cooperate	not

Let's see what you have learned from

Section 2: Avoiding the Negative:

Identification:

1. Aggression and violence
2. Controlling wrong thoughts

Clarification:

3. Explain why we need to avoid the company of friends who mislead us from the Straight Path.

Section 3: Misdeeds Bring Pain

1. The plotting of evil ensnares none but those who plot it (35:43).

lā yaḥīqul-makrus-sayyīᵓ illā bi-ahlihī

لَا يَحِيقُ الْمَكْرُ السَّيِّئُ إِلَّا بِأَهْلِهِ

bi-ahlihī	*illā*	*as-sayyīᵓ*	*al-makru*	*yaḥīqu*	*lā*
(to) its people	except(of)	evil	(the) plotting	overcomes	not

2. Whoever works a weight of a speck of dust of evil shall see it (99:8).

may-yaᶜmal mithqāla dharratin sharray yarahu

مَن يَعْمَلْ مِثْقَالَ ذَرَّةٍ شَرًّا يَرَهُ

yarahu	*sharran*	*dharratin*	*mithqāla*	*yaᶜmal*	*man*
shall see it	in evil	a speck of dust	a weight (of)	works	he who

3. Whoever earns evil has surrounded himself with his sin;

man kasaba sayyiᵓataw-wa aḥāṭat bihi khaṭīᵓatuhu

مَن كَسَبَ سَيِّئَةً وَّأَحَٰطَتْ بِهِۦ خَطِيٓـَٔتُهُۥ

khaṭīᵓatuhu	*bihi*	*aḥāṭat*	*wa*	*sayyiᵓatin*	*kasaba*	*man*
his sin	(with) him	his surrounded	and	evil	earns	he who

they are then the companions of the fire dwelling forever in it (2:81).

fa-ūlāᵓika aṣḥābun-nār hum fīhā khālidūn

فَأُولَٰٓئِكَ أَصْحَٰبُ النَّارِ ۖ هُمْ فِيهَا خَٰلِدُونَ

khālidūn	*fīhā*	*hum*	*an-nar*	*ashabu*	*fa-ūlāᵓika*
dwelling forever	in ti	they are	the fire	(the) companions	then they (are)

4. Did those who commit misdeeds imagine

am ḥasibal-ladhīna-jtaraḥū-s-sayyiᵓāt

أَمْ حَسِبَ الَّذِينَ اجْتَرَحُوا السَّيِّـَٔاتِ

as-sayyiᵓāt	*jtaraḥū*	*al-ladhīna*	*ḥasiba*	*am*
misdeeds	committed	those who	did they think	?

that We shall hold them as those

an naj^{c}alahum kal-ladhīna

أَن نَّجْعَلَهُمْ كَالَّذِينَ

kal-ladhīṇna	*naj^{c}alahum*	*an*
like those who	We shall make them	that

who believe and performed good deeds

āmanū wa ^{c}amilūṣ-ṣāliḥāt

ءَامَنُوا وَعَمِلُوا الصَّٰلِحَٰتِ

aṣ-ṣāliḥāt	*^{c}amilū*	*wa*	*āmanū*
(the) good deeds	performed	and	believed

and that their living and dying are equal?

sawā^ɔ am-maḥyāhum wa mamātuhum

سَوَآءً مَّحْيَاهُمْ وَمَمَاتُهُمْ

mamātuhum	*wa*	*maḥyāhum*	*sawā^ɔ an*
their dying	and	their living	(are) equal

How poor do they judge (45:21)!

sā^{ɔ}a mā yaḥkumūn

سَآءَ مَا يَحْكُمُونَ

yaḥkumūn	*mā*	*sā^{ɔ}a*
they judge	how	poor

5. Whoever does wrong shall be punished only to that extent (40:40).

man ^{c}amila sayyi^{ɔ}atan fa-lā yujzā illā mithlahā

مَنْ عَمِلَ سَيِّئَةً فَلَا يُجْزَىٰٓ إِلَّا مِثْلَهَا

mithlahā	*illā*	*yujzā*	*fa-lā*	*sayyi^{ɔ}atan*	*^{c}amila*	*man*
its like	except with	be punished	then not	evil	performed	he who

6. The reward of an evil deed is an evil like it (42:40).

jazāʾu sayyiʾatin sayyiʾatum-mithluhā

جَزَٰٓؤُا۟ سَيِّئَةٍ سَيِّئَةٌ مِّثْلُهَا

mithluhā	*sayyiʾatun*	*sayyiʾatin*	*jazāʾu*
like it	(is) an evil	an evil deed	(the) reward of

7. He who does wrong will not

man jāʾa bis-sayyiʾati fa-lā

مَنْ جَآءَ بِالسَّيِّئَةِ فَلَا

fa-lā	*bis-sayyiʾati*	*jāʾa*	*man*
then not	with (the) evil	came	he who

be rewarded for misdeeds performed

yujzāl-ladhīna ʿamilūs-sayyiʾāt

يُجْزَى الَّذِينَ عَمِلُوا السَّيِّـَٔاتِ

as-sayyiʾāt	*ʿamilū*	*al-ladhīna*	*yujzā*
(the) misdeeds	performed	those who	be rewarded

except for what they had done (28:84).

illā mā kānū yaʿmalūn

إِلَّا مَا كَانُوا يَعْمَلُونَ

yaʿmalūn	*kānū*	*mā*	*illā*
doing	they were	what	except

8. Whoever makes an evil recommendation

may-yashfaʿ shafāʿatan sayyiʾatay

مَنْ يَّشْفَعْ شَفَٰعَةً سَيِّئَةً

sayyiʾatan	*shafāʿatan*	*yashfaʿ*	*man*
evil	a recommendation	recommends	he who

shall have a share in its burden (4:85).

-yakul-lahu kiflum minhā

يَكُن لَّهُۥ كِفْلٌ مِّنْهَا

minhā	*kiflum*	*lahu*	*yakun*
from it	a burden	for him	it will be

9. Whoever is spiritually blind in this world

man kāna-fī hādhihi a^{c}mā

مَنْ كَانَ فِي هَٰذِهِۦٓ أَعْمَىٰ

a^{c}mā	*hādhihi*	*fī*	*kāna*	*man*
blind	this	in	was	he who

will be spiritually blind in the hereafter as well and far astray from the path (17:72).

fa-huwa fil-ākhirati a^{c}mā wa aḍallu sabīlan

فَهُوَ فِي الْأٓخِرَةِ أَعْمَىٰ وَأَضَلُّ سَبِيلًا

sabīlan	*aḍallu*	*wa*	*a^{c}mā*	*al-ākhirati*	*fī*	*fa-huwa*
in the path	more astray	and	blind	the hereafter	in	then he (will be)

Let's find out what you have learned from

Section 3: Misdeeds Bring Pain:

Identification:

1. The plotting of evil ensnares who?
2. The companions of the fire.
3. Punishment for misdeeds according to 40:40.

Section 4: Lying, Backbiting and Ridiculing Others

1. Avoid falsehood (22:30).

wa-jtanibū qawlaz-zūr

وَاجْتَنِبُوا قَوْلَ الزُّورِ

az-zūr	*qawla*	*ijtanibū*	*wa*
(the) falsehood	(the) word (of)	avoid	and

2. Do not backbite against each other (49:12).

lā yaghtab ba^{c}ḍukum ba^{c}ḍan

لَا يَغْتَبْ بَعْضُكُمْ بَعْضًا

ba^{c}ḍan	*ba^{c}ḍukum*	*yaghtab*	*lā*
others	some of you	backbite	not

3. Do not be after that about which you have no

lā taqfu mā laysa laka bihi

لَا تَقْفُ مَا لَيْسَ لَكَ بِهِ

bihi	*laka*	*laysa*	*mā*	*taqfu*	*lā*
in it	for you	there is not	that	follow	not

knowledge. Truly hearing, seeing,

^{c}ilmun-innas-sam^{c}a wal-baṣara

عِلْمٌ إِنَّ السَّمْعَ وَالْبَصَرَ

al-baṣara	*wa*	*as-sam^{c}a*	*inna*	*^{c}ilmu*
(the) sight	and	(the) hearing	truly	knowledge

and the heart—each one of them

wal-fu$^{\circ}$āda kullu ūlā$^{\circ}$ika kāna

وَالْفُؤَادَ كُلُّ أُولَٰئِكَ كَانَ

kāna	*ūlā$^{\circ}$ika*	*kulla*	*al-fu$^{\circ}$āda*	*wa*
would be	them	each (of)	the heart	and

shall be questioned about it (17:36).

ᶜanhu masᵓūlan

عَنْهُ مَسْـُٔولًا

masᵓūlan	*ᶜanhu*
questioned	about it

4. He who commits a fault or a sin

may-yaksib khaṭiᵓatan aw ithman

مَن يَكْسِبْ خَطِيٓـَٔةً أَوْ إِثْمًا

ithman	*aw*	*khaṭiᵓatan*	*yaksib*	*man*
sin	or	misdeed	earns	he who

then throws (its blame) on an innocent person,

thumma yarmi bihi barīᵓan faqadi-

ثُمَّ يَرْمِ بِهِۦ بَرِيٓـًٔا فَقَدِ

faqad	*barīᵓan*	*bihi*	*yarmi*	*thumma*
he has indeed	(on) an innocent person	(with) it	throws	then

he certainly burdens himself with a falsehood and a manifest sin (4:112).

-ḥtamala buhtānaw-wa ithmam mubīnan

ٱحْتَمَلَ بُهْتَٰنًا وَإِثْمًا مُّبِينًا

mubīnan	*ithman*	*wa*	*buhtānan*	*iḥtamala*
clear	sin	and	slander	borne

5. Those who annoy the believing men

wal-ladhīna yūᵓdhūnal-muᵓminīn

وَٱلَّذِينَ يُؤْذُونَ ٱلْمُؤْمِنِينَ

al-muᵓminīn	*yūᵓdhūn*	*wal-ladhīna*
the believing men	annoy	and those who

and the believing women undeserevedly:

wal-muᵓmināt bighayri mā-ktasabū

وَالْمُؤْمِنٰتِ بِغَيْرِ مَا اكْتَسَبُوا

iktasabū	*mā*	*bighayri*	*al-muᵓmināt*	*wa*
they deserve	what	without	the believing women	and

they have indeed borne slander and sin (33:58).

faqadi-ḥtamalū buhtānaw-wa ithmam-mubinan

فَقَدِ احْتَمَلُوا بُهْتٰنًا وَّإِثْمًا مُّبِينًا

ithman	*wa*	*buhtānan*	*iḥtamalū*	*faqad*
sin	and	slander	borne	they have indeed

6. If a sinner has come to you with a report then ascertain the truth

in jāᵓakum fāsiqun-binabāᵓin fa-tabayyanū

إِنْ جَآءَكُمْ فَاسِقٌۢ بِنَبَإٍ فَتَبَيَّنُوٓا

fa-tabayyanū	*binabāᵓin*	*fāsiqun*	*jāᵓakum*	*in*
then ascertain the truth	with a report	a sinner	has come to you	if

lest you injure a people in ignorance

an tuṣībū qawman bi-jahālatin

أَنْ تُصِيبُوا قَوْمًا بِجَهٰلَةٍ

bi-jahālatin	*qawman*	*tuṣībū*	*an*
in ignorance	a people	you injure	lest

and regret what you did (49:6).

fa-tuṣbihū ᶜalā mā faᶜaltum nādimīn

فَتُصْبِحُوا عَلٰى مَا فَعَلْتُمْ نٰدِمِينَ

nādimīn	*faᶜaltum*	*mā*	*ᶜalā*	*fa-tuṣbihū*
regretters	you did	what	on	and become

7. *Let not a people mock another, perhaps*

lā yaskhar qawwum-min qawmin ^{c}asā

لَا يَسْخَرْ قَوْمٌ مِّنْ قَوْمٍ عَسٰٓى

^{c}asā	*qawmin*	*min*	*qawmun*	*yaskhar*	*lā*
perhaps	a people	(of)	a people	mock	not

perchance the latter may be better than the former.

ay-yakūnū khayram-minhum wa

أَنْ يَّكُوْنُوْا خَيْرًا مِّنْهُمْ وَ

wa	*minhum*	*kayran*	*yakūnū*	*an*
and	than they	better	they are	(that)

Nor let some women mock other women,

lā nisāʾʾum-min nisāʾin ^{c}asā ay-

لَا نِسَآءٌ مِّنْ نِّسَآءٍ عَسٰٓى أَنْ

an	*^{c}asā*	*nisāʾ*	*min*	*nisāʾ*	*lā*
(that)	perhaps	women	(of)	women	not

it may be that the latter are better than the former.

-yakunna khayram minhunna wa lā

يَّكُنَّ خَيْرًا مِّنْهُنَّ ج وَلَا

lā	*wa*	*minhunna*	*khayran*	*yakunna*
not	and	than they	better	they are

Do not defame or insult each other

talmizū anfusakum wa lā tanābazū

تَلْمِزُوْٓا أَنْفُسَكُمْ وَلَا تَنَابَزُوْا

tanābazū	*lā*	*wa*	*anfusakum*	*talmizū*
insult each other	not	and	yourselves	defame

nor call each other by (offensive) nicknames. Bad is the name of wickedness

bil-alqābi biʾsal-ismul-fusūq

بِالْأَلْقَٰبِ بِئْسَ الِاسْمُ الْفُسُوقُ

al-fusūq	*al-ismu*	*biʾsa*	*bil-alqābi*
the wicked	the name (of)	it is bad	with nicknames

after faith (49:11).

baʿdal-īmān

بَعْدَ الْإِيمَٰنِ

al-īmān	*baʿda*
(the) belief	after

Let's find out what you have learned from

Section 4: Lying, Backbiting, Ridiculing Others:

Identification:

1. Falsehood
2. Backbiting

Clarification:

3. Explain what the Quran says about using bad language (49:11).

Section 5: Boasting, Arrogance and Showing Off

1. Truly He loves not the arrogant (16:23).

innahu lā yuḥibbul-mustakbirīn

إِنَّهُ لَا يُحِبُّ الْمُسْتَكْبِرِينَ

al-mustakbirīn	*yuḥibbu*	*lā*	*innahu*
the arrogant	loves	not	truly He

2. Truly God loves not him who is conceited and boastful (4:36).

inna-llāha lā yuḥibbu man kāna mukhtālan fakhūr

إِنَّ اللَّهَ لَا يُحِبُّ مَنْ كَانَ مُخْتَالًا فَخُورًا

fakhūr	*mukhtālan*	*kāna*	*man*	*yuḥibbu*	*lā*	*Allāh*	*inna*
boastful	conceited	was	him who	loves	not	God	truly

3. Walk not on the earth exultant!

lā tamshi fil-^{c}arḍi maraḥan

لَا تَمْشِ فِي الْأَرْضِ مَرَحًا

maraḥan	*al-^{c}arḍ*	*fī*	*tamshī*	*lā*
exultant	the earth	on	walk	not

Truly you will not tear apart the earth and

innaka lan takhriqal-^{c}arḍ wa

إِنَّكَ لَنْ تَخْرِقَ الْأَرْضَ وَ

wa	*al-^{c}arḍ*	*takhriq*	*lan*	*innaka*
and	the earth	tear apart	will not	truly you

will not reach the mountains in height (17:37).

lan tablughal-jibāla ṭūlan

لَنْ تَبْلُغَ الْجِبَالَ طُولًا

ṭūlan	*al-jibāl*	*tablugh*	*lan*
in height	the mountains	reach	will not

4. Do not look contemptuously at people (31:18).

lā tuṣa^{cc}ir khaddaha lin-nās

لَا تُصَعِّرْ خَدَّكَ لِلنَّاسِ

lin-nās	*khaddaka*	*tuṣa^{cc}ir*	*lā*
to (the) people	your cheek	look at	not

5. As for those who scorned and were haughty , Lo!

ammāl-ladhīna stankafū wa-stakbarū

أَمَّا الَّذِينَ اسْتَنكَفُوا وَ اسْتَكْبَرُوا

istakbarū	*wa*	*istankafū*	*al-ladhīna*	*ammā*
were haughty	and	scorned	those who	as for

He will punish them a painful punishing (4:173).

fa-yu^{c}adhdhibuhum ^{c}adhāban alīman

فَيُعَذِّبُهُمْ عَذَابًا أَلِيمًا

alīman	*^{c}adhāban*	*fa-yu^{c}adhdhibuhum*
painful	a punishing	lo! He will punish them

Let's see what you have learned from

Section 5: Boasting, Arrogance and Showing Off:

Identification:

1. Arrogant
2. Boastful

Clarification:

3. Explain how someone walks upon the earth indolently.

Section 6: Mischief-Making

1. God loves not immorality (2:205).

allāhu lā yuḥibbul-fasād

اللّٰهُ لَا يُحِبُّ الْفَسَادَ

al-fasād	*yuḥibbu*	*lā*	*Allāh*
(the) immorality	loves	not	God

2. Do not wish for immorality on the earth (28:77).

lā tabghil-fasād fīl-^{c}arḍ

لَا تَبْغِ الْفَسَادَ فِي الْأَرْضِ

al-^{c}arḍ	*fī*	*al-fasād*	*tabghi*	*lā*
the earth	on	(the) immorality	wish for	not

3. Act not wickedly on the earth as corrupters (2:60).

lā ta^{c}thaw fīl-^{c}arḍ mufsidīn

لَا تَعْثَوْا فِي الْأَرْضِ مُفْسِدِينَ

mufsidīn	*al-^{c}arḍ*	*fī*	*ta^{c}thaw*	*lā*
as corrupters	the earth	on	act wickedly	not

4. God loves not the immoral (5:64).

allāhu lā yuḥibbul-mufsidīn

اللّٰهُ لَا يُحِبُّ الْمُفْسِدِينَ

al-mufsidīn	*yuḥibbu*	*lā*	*Allāh*
the immoral	loves	not	God

5. Truly God loves the just (5:42).

inna-llāha yuḥibbul-muqsiṭīn

إِنَّ اللّٰهَ يُحِبُّ الْمُقْسِطِينَ

al-muqsiṭīn	*yuḥibbu*	*Allāh*	*inna*
the fair	loves	God	truly

6. Truly God commands justice and

inna-llaha yaᵓmuru bil-ᶜadl wa-

إِنَّ اللَّهَ يَأْمُرُ بِالْعَدْلِ وَ

wa	*bil-ᶜadl*	*yaᵓmuru*	*Allāh*	*inna*
and	(with the) justice	commands	God	truly

goodness and generosity to kinsmen

-l-iḥsān wa ītāᵓi dhīl-qurbā

الْإِحْسَٰنِ وَإِيتَآئِ ذِي الْقُرْبَىٰ

dhīl-qurbā	*ītāᵓi*	*wa*	*al-iḥsān*
to kinsmen	(the) giving	and	(the) goodness

and forbids lewdness, wrongdoing, and injustice (16:90).

wa yanhā ᶜanil-faḥshāᵓi wal-munkiri wal-baghyi

وَيَنْهَىٰ عَنِ الْفَحْشَآءِ وَالْمُنْكَرِ وَالْبَغْيِ

al-baghyi	*wa*	*al-munkir*	*wa*	*al-faḥshāᵓi*	*ᶜani*	*yanhā*
(the) injustice	and	(the) wrongdoing	and	(the) lewdness	(from)	forbids

7. Truly those who tempt the believing men

innal-ladhīna fatanūl-muᵓminīn

إِنَّ الَّذِينَ فَتَنُوا الْمُؤْمِنِينَ

al-muᵓminīn	*fatanū*	*al-ladhīna*	*inna*
the believing men	tempted	those who	truly

and the believing women and do not repent,

wal-muᵓmināt thummā lam yatūbū

وَالْمُؤْمِنَٰتِ ثُمَّ لَمْ يَتُوبُوا

yatūbū	*lam*	*thummā*	*al-muᵓmināt*	*wa*
repent	did not	then	the believing women	and

for them shall be the torment of hell

fa-lahum ʿadhābu jahannam wa lahum

فَلَهُمْ عَذَابُ جَهَنَّمَ وَلَهُمْ

lahum	*wa*	*jahannam*	*ʿadhābu*	*fa-lahum*
for them	and	(of) hell	(the) punishment	(then) for them (is)

and the torment of burning (85:10).

ʿadhābul-ḥarīq

عَذَابُ الْحَرِيقِ

al-ḥarīq	*ʿadhābu*
of the burning	(the) torment

8. Hold fast to God's rope all together and do not be disunited (3:103).

wa-ʿtaṣimū bi-ḥabli-llāhi jamīʿan wa lā tafarraqū

عْتَصِمُوا بِحَبْلِ اللَّهِ جَمِيعًا وَّلَا تَفَرَّقُوا ص

tafarraqū	*ḷā*	*wa*	*jamīʿan*	*Allah*	*bi-habli*	*iʿtaṣimū*	*wa*
disperse	not	and	all	of God	to the rope	hold fast	and

9. Do not quarrel for you will despair and

lā tanāzaʿū fa-tafshalū wa

لَا تَنَازَعُوا فَتَفْشَلُوا وَ

wa	*fa-tafshalū*	*tanāzaʿū*	*lā*
and	for you will despair	quarrel	not

your strength will go (8:46).

tadhhab rīḥukum

تَذْهَبَ رِيحُكُمْ

rīḥukum	*tadhhab*
your strength	will go

Let's find out what you have learned from

Section 6: Mischief-Making:

Identification:

1. Which chapter and verse forbids corruption on the earth?
2. Just people

Clarification:

3. Explain from 16:90 what God commands and what God forbids.

Section 7: Oppression

1. God does not like the oppressors (3:57).

allāhu lā yuḥibbuẓ-ẓālimīn

اللَّهُ لَا يُحِبُّ الظَّٰلِمِينَ

aẓ-ẓālimīn	*yuḥibbu*	*lā*	*Allāh*
the oppressors	loves	not	God

2. Truly do not exceed the bounds; God does not

lā ta^{c}tadū-inna-llāha lā

لَا تَعْتَدُوا إِنَّ اللَّهَ لَا

lā	*Allāh*	*inna*	*ta^{c}tadū*	*lā*
not	God	truly	overstep	not

love the aggressors (5:87).

yuḥibbul-mu^{c}tadīn

يُحِبُّ الْمُعْتَدِينَ

mu^{c}tadīn	*yuḥibbu*
the aggressors	loves

3. Consider not God neglectful of what the oppressors do (14:42).

lā taḥsabana-llāha ghāfilan ^{c}ammā ya^{c}maluẓ-ẓālimūn

لَا تَحْسَبَنَّ اللَّهَ غَٰفِلًا عَمَّا يَعْمَلُ الظَّٰلِمُونَ

aẓ-ẓālimūn	*ya^{c}malu*	*^{c}ammā*	*ghāfilan*	*Allāh*	*taḥsabana*	*lā*
the oppressors	perform	of what	neglectful	God	consider	not

4. Oppress not and be not oppressed (2:279).

lā taẓlimūn wa lā tuẓlamūn

لَا تَظْلِمُونَ وَلَا تُظْلَمُونَ

tuẓlamūn	*lā*	*wa*	*taẓlimūn*	*lā*
be oppressed	not	and	oppress	not

5. Act not wickedly on the earth as do the immoral (26:183).

lā ta^{c}thaw fīl-arḍ mufsidīn

لَا تَعْثَوْا فِي الْأَرْضِ مُفْسِدِينَ

mufsidīn	*al-^{c}arḍ*	*fī*	*ta^{c}thaw*	*lā*
as the immoral	the earth	on	act wickedly	not

Let's find out what you have learned from

Section 7: Oppression:

Fill in the blanks:

1. Wrong not and _______ (2:279).

Identification:

2. Oppressor (5:87)

Section 8: Cheating and Stealing

1. Do not devour your wealth among yourselves in vanity (2:188).

lā ta°kulū amwālakum baynakum bil-bāṭil

لَا تَأْكُلُوٓاْ أَمْوَٰلَكُمْ بَيْنَكُمْ بِٱلْبَٰطِلِ

bil-bāṭil	*baynakum*	*amwālakum*	*ta°kulu*	*lā*
vainly	among you	your goods	consume	not

2. Do not defraud people of their things (26:183)

lā tabkhasūn-nās ashyāhum

لَا تَبْخَسُواْ ٱلنَّاسَ أَشْيَآءَهُمْ

ashyāhum	*an-nās*	*tabkhasū*	*lā*
their things	the people	lessen	not

Let's find out what you have learned from

Section 8: Cheating and Stealing:

Identification:

1. Explain false ways we can use our wealth.

Section 9: Extravagance and Squandering

1. Be not extravagant. Truly He loves not the extravagant (6:141).

lā tusrifūinnahu lā yuḥibbu-l-musrifīn

لَا تُسْرِفُوا ۚ إِنَّهُ لَا يُحِبُّ الْمُسْرِفِينَ

al-musrifīn	*yuḥibbu*	*la*	*innahu*	*tusrifū*	*lā*
the extravagant	loves	not	truly He	be extravagant	not

2. Do not squander wastefully (17:26).

lā tubadhdhir tabdhiran

لَا تُبَذِّرْ تَبْذِيرًا

tabdhiran	*tubadhdhir*	*lā*
wastefully	squander	not

3. Truly the squanderers were the brothers of the satans (17:27).

innal-mubadhdhirīn kānū ikhwānash-shayāṭīn

إِنَّ الْمُبَذِّرِينَ كَانُوا إِخْوَانَ الشَّيَاطِينِ

ash-shayāṭīn	*ikhwān*	*kānū*	*al-mubadhdhirīn*	*inna*
the satans	the brothers (of)	were	the squanderers	truly

4. Obey not the order of the extravagant (26:151).

lā tuṭīᶜū amral-musrifīn

لَا تُطِيعُوا أَمْرَ الْمُسْرِفِينَ

al-musrifīn	*amra*	*tuṭīᶜū*	*lā*
the extravagant	(the) order (of)	obey	not

Let's find out what you have learned from

Section 9: Extravagance and Squandering:
Identification:
1. Squanderers (17:27)

Section 10: Misappropriation and Embezzlement

1. Truly God commands you to return

inna-llāha yaʾmurukum an tuʿaddū-

إِنَّ اللَّهَ يَأْمُرُكُمْ أَنْ تُؤَدُّوا

tuʿaddū	*an*	*yaʾmurukum*	*Allah*	*inna*
return	to	commands you	God	truly

trusts in deposit to their owners (4:58).

-l-amānāt ilā ahlihā

الْأَمَٰنَٰتِ إِلَىٰٓ أَهْلِهَا

ahlihā	*ilā*	*al-amānāt*
its owners	to	the deposits in trust

2. Truly God loves not the betrayers (8:58).

inna-l-lāha lā yuḥibbul-khāʾinīn

إِنَّ اللَّهَ لَا يُحِبُّ الْخَآئِنِينَ

al-khāʾinīn	*yuḥibbu*	*lā*	*Allāh*	*inna*
the betrayers	loves	not	God	truly

Let's find out what you have learned from

Section 10: Misappropriation and Embezzlement:

Identification:

1. Trusts (4:58).
2. Embezzlers (8:58).

Section 11: Mischievous Thoughts

1. Follow not lust! (4:135).

lā tattabi^{c}ūl-hawā

لَا تَتَّبِعُوا الْهَوَىٰ

al-hawā	*attabi^{c}ū*	*lā*
(the) lust	follow	not

2. Whoever dreaded standing before his Lord

man khāfa maqāma rabbihi

مَنْ خَافَ مَقَامَ رَبِّهِ

rabbihi	*maqāma*	*khāfa*	*man*
his Lord	(his) place (by)	feared	he who

and restrained the appetite from the whim of passion

wa nahān-nafsa ^{c}anil-hawā

وَنَهَى النَّفْسَ عَنِ الْهَوَىٰ

al-hawā	*^{c}ani*	*an-nafsa*	*nahā*	*wa*
(the) whim of passion	for	the appetite	restrained	and

then truly paradise will be his abode (79:40-41).

fa-innal-jannata hiyal-ma^{ↄ}wā

فَإِنَّ الْجَنَّةَ هِيَ الْمَأْوَىٰ

al-ma^{ↄ}wā	*hiya*	*al-jannata*	*fa-inna*
the abode	it (will be)	the garden	then truly

3. Avoid too much suspicion.

ijtanibū kathīran minaẓ-ẓanni

اجْتَنِبُوا كَثِيرًا مِّنَ الظَّنِّ

aẓ-ẓanni	*min*	*kathiṛan*	*ijtanibū*
(the) suspicion	of	much	avoid

Truly some suspicion is a sin (49:12).

inna ba^cḍaẓ-ẓanni ithmun

إِنَّ بَعْضَ الظَّنِّ إِثْمٌ

ithmun	*aẓ-ẓanni*	*ba^cḍa*	*inna*
a sin	(the) suspicion (is)	some (of)	truly

4. He who is given wisdom has been granted

may-yu^ɔtal-ḥikmata faqad ūtiya

مَنْ يُؤْتَ الْحِكْمَةَ فَقَدْ أُوتِيَ

ūtiya	*faqad*	*al-ḥikmata*	*yu^ɔta*	*man*
granted	he has been	(the) wisdom	is given	he who

much good (2:269).

khayran kathīran

خَيْرًا كَثِيرًا

kathīran	*khayran*
much	good

Let's find out what you have learned from

Section 11: Mischievous Thoughts:

Identification:

1. Lustful thoughts (79:40-41).
2. Being suspicious (49:12).

Section 12: Misleading Friends

1. Turn away from the ignorant (7:199).

a^{c}riḍ ^{c}anil-jāhilīn

وَأَعْرِضْ عَنِ الْجٰهِلِيْنَ

al-jāhilīn	*^{c}ani*	*a^{c}riḍ*
the ignorant	from	turn away

2. God save me from being of the ignorant (2:67).

a^{c}ūdhu billāhi an akūn mina-l-jāhilīn

أَعُوذُ بِاللهِ أَنْ أَكُونَ مِنَ الْجٰهِلِيْنَ

al-jāhilīn	*min*	*akūn*	*an*	*billāhi*	*a^{c}ūdhu*
the ignorant	of	I should be	that	with God	I take refuge

3. Join me with the righteous (26:83).

alḥiqnī biṣ-ṣāliḥīn

أَلْحِقْنِي بِالصّٰلِحِيْنَ

biṣ-ṣāliḥīn	*alḥiqnī*
with the righteous	join me

Let's find out what you have learned from

Section 12: Misleading Friends:

Identification:

1. Take refuge with God... (7:199).

Section 13: Conclusion

Negative traits the Quran counsels us to avoid include lying, backbiting, and ridiculing others; boasting, arrogance and showing-off; mischief-making, oppression, cheating and stealing; extravagance and squandering; misappropriation and embezzlement; mischievous thoughts and following misleading friends. These are all traits that believers try to avoid at all costs because it brings about God's displeasure. It is to show ingratitude in face of the life He has given us.

Section Answers:

Section 2: Avoiding the Negative

1. Must be avoided at all costs.
2. This is essential for the wholesome growth of our character and personality.
3. Each response differs.

Section 3: Misdeeds Bring Pain

1. Those who plot evil.
2 Whoever does evil.
3. To the extent of the evil.

Section 4: Lying, Backbiting, and Ridiculing Others

1. avoid it (22:30).
2. avoid it (49:12).
3. Each response differs.

Section 5: Boasting, Arrogance and Showing Off

1. God loves him (her) not (16:23).
2. God loves him (her) not (4:36).
3. Each response differs.

Section 6: Mischief-Making

1. (28:77)
2. God loves them (5:42).
3. Commands: Justice, goodness and helping relatives.
Forbids: Indecency, wickedness and rebellion.

Section 7: Oppression

1. You shall not be wronged (2:279).
2. Someone who exceeds God's bounds.

Section 8: Cheating and Stealing

1. Each response differs.

Section 9: Extravagance and Squandering

1. Brothers of satan (17:27).

Section 10: Misappropriation and Embezzlement

1. Return to their owners (4:58).
2. God does not like them (8:58).

Section 11: Mischievous Thoughts

1. Doing what our passions tell us to do.
2. Avoid it.

Section 12: Misleading Friends

1. ...from the ignorant (7:199).

6
Self-Development

Section 1: Introduction

The Quran encourages us to put aside despair and depression. To be depressed means we are not appreciating the blessings He has given us. That is, we are not grateful to Him. God provided us with the possibilities to develop our full potential to complete our nature He originated (*fitrat Allah*) (See 30:30).

To err is human. We are all liable to commit errors and omissions despite our very best wishes to keep away from them. What should you do when an arrow has been shot in the wrong direction? Kill all hope and start crying? Dive deep into the depths of despair? Lose heart and stop toiling? Obviously not! That will make matters worse. Would you adopt a reckless attitude and go on committing error after error senselessly? That would, indeed, be doubly harmful.

What then should a child do? The Quran offers wholesome guidance in this significant field of life, as well. It is full of charming verses which motivate people to hard work. These marvellous verses have been responsible for the most creative developments in human history. They strike at the very roots of depression and despair. Our body and mind become reinvigorated for improved effort. They kindle the light of hope and confidence. They thus enable us to face the struggle for life more and more energetically. Indeed it is these very verses which possess the magic powers of turning even the most useless persons into self-confident individuals and constructive citizens.

These energizing verses have been discussed here under the following headings:

Section 2: Dispel Despair and Depression

No worthwhile achievement is possible if we do not cover over our disappointments and depressions. Life demands hope and confidence, that is, a positive state of mind.

Section 3: Self-Development

It is never too late to start thinking and working properly. We must labor hard for all-round improvement and progress.

Section 4: Conclusion

Section 2: Dispel Despair and Depression

1. Despair not of God's Mercy!

lā taqnaṭū mir-raḥmati-llāhi

لَا تَقْنَطُوا مِن رَّحْمَةِ اللَّهِ

Allāh	*raḥmati*	*min*	*taqnaṭū*	*lā*
(of) God	(the) mercy	of	despair	not

Truly God forgives sins entirely (39:53).

inna-llāha yaghfirudh-dhunūba jami^{c}an

إِنَّ اللَّهَ يَغْفِرُ الذُّنُوبَ جَمِيعًا

jami^{c}an	*adh-dhunūba*	*yaghfir*	*Allāh*	*inna*
entirely	the sins	forgives	God	truly

2. Be not of the desponding (15:55).

lā takum-minal-qāniṭīn

لَا تَكُن مِّنَ الْقَٰنِطِينَ

al-qāniṭīn	*min*	*takun*	*lā*
the despairers	of	be	not

3. God is with you and will never deprive you of your (good) deeds (47:35).

wallahu ma^{c}akum wa lay-yatirakum a^{c}mālakum

وَاللَّهُ مَعَكُمْ وَلَن يَتِرَكُمْ أَعْمَٰلَكُمْ

a^{c}mālakum	*yatirakum*	*lan*	*wa*	*ma^{c}akum*	*Allāh*
(of) your deeds	wrong you	He will not	and	(is) with you	God

4. Do not lose heart nor grieve!

lā tahinū wa lā tahzanū

لَا تَهِنُوا وَلَا تَحْزَنُوا وَ

tahzanū	*lā*	*wa*	*tahinū*	*lā*
grieve	not	and	lose heart	not

You shall triumph if you are believers (3:139).

wa antumul-aʿlawna in kuntum muʾminīn

وَأَنتُمُ الْأَعْلَوْنَ إِن كُنتُم مُّؤْمِنِينَ

muʾminīn	*kuntum*	*in*	*al-aʿlawna*	*antum*	*wa*
believers	you were	if	the overcomers	you (are)	and

5. Whoever believes in his Lord fears not

may-yuʾmim-birabbihi fa-lā yakhāfu

مَن يُؤْمِن بِرَبِّهِ فَلَا يَخَافُ

yakhāfu	*fa-lā*	*birabbihi*	*yuʾmin*	*man*
he fears	then not	in his Lord	believes	he who

loss or oppression (72:13).

bakhsaw-wa lā rahaqan

بَخْسًا وَلَا رَهَقًا

rahaqan	*lā*	*wa*	*bakhsan*
oppression	not	and	loss

6. No kind of calamity befalls except with God's leave.

mā aṣāba mim-muṣībatin illā bi-idhnil-lāhi

مَا أَصَابَ مِن مُّصِيبَةٍ إِلَّا بِإِذْنِ اللَّهِ

Allāh	*bi-idhni*	*illā*	*muṣībatin*	*min*	*aṣāba*	*mā*
God	with permission (of)	except	calamity	of	afflicted	not

Whoever believes in God He guides his heart (aright) (64:11).

wa may-yūʾmim billāhi yahdi qalbahu

وَمَن يُؤْمِن بِاللَّهِ يَهْدِ قَلْبَهُ

qalbahu	*yahdi*	*billāhi*	*yūʾmin*	*man*	*wa*
his heart	He guides	in God	believes	he who	and

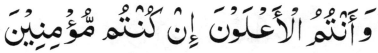

7. *Whosoever believes and reforms (his life),*

man āmana wa aṣlaḥa

مَنْ ءَامَنَ وَأَصْلَحَ

aṣlaḥa	*wa*	*āmana*	*man*
reformed	and	believed	he who

on such people shall come no fear nor shall they grieve (6:48).

fa-lā khawfun ^{c}alayhim wa lā hum yaḥzanūn

فَلَا خَوْفٌ عَلَيْهِمْ وَلَا هُمْ يَحْزَنُونَ

yaḥzanūn	*hum*	*lā*	*wa*	*^{c}alayhim*	*khawfun*	*fa-lā*
grieve	they	not	and	on them	fear	(then there is) not

8. *Those who fear God and act righteously,*

man ittaqā wa aṣlaḥa fa-lā khawfun

مَنِ اتَّقَىٰ وَأَصْلَحَ فَلَا خَوْفٌ

khawfun	*fa-lā*	*aṣlaḥa*	*wa*	*ittaqā*	*man*
fear	(then there is) not	reformed	and	feared (God)	he who

they shall not fear nor shall they grieve (7:35).

^{c}alayhim wa lā hum yaḥzanūn

عَلَيْهِمْ وَلَا هُمْ يَحْزَنُونَ

yaḥzanūn	*hum*	*lā*	*wa*	*^{c}alayhim*
grieve	they	not	and	on them

9. *Whoever does good deeds*

may-ya^{c}mal minaṣ-ṣaliḥat

مَنْ يَعْمَلْ مِنَ الصَّٰلِحَٰتِ

aṣ-ṣaliḥat	*min*	*ya^{c}mal*	*man*
(the) good deeds	of	performs	he who

and a believer shall have no fear

wa huwa muᵓmin fa-lā yakhāfu

وَهُوَ مُؤْمِنٌ فَلَا يَخَافُ

yakhāfu	*fa-lā*	*muᵓmin*	*huwa*	*wa*
he fears	then not	a believer	he (is)	and

of oppression and long-suffering (20:112).

ẓulmaw-wa lā haḍman

ظُلْمًا وَلَا هَضْمًا

haḍman	*lā*	*wa*	*ẓulma*
long-suffering	not	and	oppression

10. Whoever submits himself to God and

man aslama wajhahu lillāhi wa

مَنْ أَسْلَمَ وَجْهَهُ لِلَّهِ وَ

wa	*lillāhi*	*wajhahu*	*aslama*	*man*
and	to God	his face	submitted	he who

is a doer of good, his reward

huwa muḥsinun fa-lahu ajruhu

هُوَ مُحْسِنٌ فَلَهُ أَجْرُهُ

ajruhu	*fa-lahu*	*muḥsinun*	*huwa*
his reward	then for him	a doer of good	he (is)

is with his Lord; no fear shall come on such people,

ᶜinda rabbihi wa lā khawfun

عِنْدَ رَبِّهِ وَلَا خَوْفٌ

khawfun	*la*	*wa*	*rabbihi*	*ᶜinda*
fear	no	and	his Lord	(is) with

nor shall they grieve (2:112).

^{c}alayhim wa lā hum yaḥzanūn

عَلَيْهِمْ وَلَا هُمْ يَحْزَنُونَ

yaḥzanūn	*hum*	*lā*	*wa*	*^{c}alayhim*
grieve	they	not	and	upon them

11. Whoever believes in God and the Last Day

man āmana billāhi wal-yawmil-ākhiri

مَنْ آمَنَ بِاللّٰهِ وَالْيَوْمِ الْآخِرِ

al-ākhir	*al-yawmi*	*wa*	*billāhi*	*āmana*	*man*
(the) Last	the Day	and	in God	believed	he who

and does good; they shall not fear

wa ^{c}amila ṣāliḥan fa-lā khawfun

وَعَمِلَ صٰلِحًا فَلَا خَوْفٌ

khawfun	*fa-la*	*ṣāliḥan*	*^{c}amila*	*wa*
fear	then (there is no)	good	did	and

nor shall they grieve (5:69).

^{c}alayhim wa lā hum yaḥzanūn

عَلَيْهِمْ وَلَا هُمْ يَحْزَنُونَ

yaḥzanūn	*hum*	*lā*	*wa*	*^{c}alayhim*
grieve	they	not	and	on them

12. Truly with every difficulty there is ease (94:6).

inna ma^{c}al-^{c}usri yusran

إِنَّ مَعَ الْعُسْرِ يُسْرًا

yusran	*al-^{c}usri*	*ma^{c}a*	*inna*
is ease	(the) difficulty	with	truly

Let's find out what you have learned from

Section 2: Dispel Despair and Depression:

Fill in the blanks:

1. Do not lose heart nor grieve __________ (3:139).
2. Whoever believes in ______ (72:13).
3. Truly with every difficulty _________ (94:6).

Section 3: Self-Development

1. And seek God's forgiveness! Truly God is much Forgiving and Merciful (2:199).

wa-staghfirū-llāha inna-llāha ghafūrur-raḥīm

وَٱسْتَغْفِرُوا ٱللَّهَ إِنَّ ٱللَّهَ غَفُورٌ رَّحِيمٌ

raḥīm	*ghafūrun*	*Allāha*	*inna*	*Allāh*	*istaghfiru*	*wa*
merciful	much-forgiving	God (is)	truly	(from) God	seek forgiveness	and

2. Turn to God with a sincere repentance (66:8).

tūbū ilāllāhi tawbatan naṣūḥan

تُوبُوٓا إِلَى ٱللَّهِ تَوْبَةً نَّصُوحًا

naṣūḥan	*tawbatan*	*Allāh*	*ilā*	*tūbū*
sincere	a repentance	God	to	repent

3. If you come to a friendly understanding and fear God,

in tuṣliḥū wa tattaqū fa-inna-

إِن تُصْلِحُوا وَتَتَّقُوا فَإِنَّ

fa-inna	*tattaqū*	*wa*	*tuṣliḥū*	*in*
then truly	fear (God)	and	you settle (something)	if

then God is ever Forgiving and Merciful (4:129).

-llaha kāna ghafūrar-raḥīm

ٱللَّهَ كَانَ غَفُورًا رَّحِيمًا

raḥīm	*ghafūran*	*kāna*	*Allāh*
merciful	much-forgiving	would be	God

4. If you repent, it is better for you (9:3).

in tubtum fa-huwa khayrul-lakum

إِن تُبْتُمْ فَهُوَ خَيْرٌ لَّكُمْ

lakum	*khayrun*	*fa-huwa*	*tubtum*	*in*
for you	better	then it (would be)	you repented	if

5. *Whosoever repents, believes*

mantāba wa āmana wa

مَنْ تَابَ وَ أٰمَنَ وَ

wa	*āmana*	*wa*	*tāba*	*man*
and	believed	and	repented	he who

and does good deeds,

^{c}amila ṣāliḥan fa^{c}asā ay-

عَمِلَ صٰلِحًا فَعَسٰٓى أَنْ

an	*fa^{c}asā*	*ṣāliḥan*	*^{c}amila*
(that)	then perhaps	good	did

he shall be among the successful (28:67).

-yakun minal-mufliḥīn

يَّكُونَ مِنَ الْمُفْلِحِينَ

al-mufliḥīn	*min*	*yakun*
the successful	among	he will be

6. Whoever follows My guidance shall neither be lost

mani-ttaba^{c}a hudāya fa-lā yaḍillu

مَنِ اتَّبَعَ هُدَايَ فَلَا يَضِلُّ

yaḍillu	*fa-lā*	*hudāya*	*ittaba^{c}a*	*man*
is lost	then not	My guidance	followed	he who

nor be wretched (20:123).

wa lā yashqā

وَلَا يَشْقٰى

yashqā	*lā*	*wa*
he is wretched	not	and

7. *Whoever pardons and makes reconciliation,*

man ᶜafā wa aṣlaḥa

مَنْ عَفَا وَأَصْلَحَ

aṣlaḥa	*wa*	*ᶜafā*	*man*
reconciliated	and	pardoned	he who

his reward is due from God (42:40).

fa-ajruhu ᶜalāl-lāh

فَأَجْرُهُ عَلَى اللَّهِ

Allāh	*ᶜalā*	*fa-ajruhu*
God	on	then his reward (is)

8. *He is the One who accepts repentance*

huwal-ladhī yaqbalut-tawba

هُوَ الَّذِي يَقْبَلُ التَّوْبَةَ

at-tawba	*yaqbalu*	*al-ladhī*	*huwa*
(the) repentance	accepts	the One who	He is

from His worshippers and pardons evil deeds (42:25).

ᶜan ᶜibādihi wa yaᶜfū ᶜanis-sayyiāt

عَنْ عِبَادِهِ وَيَعْفُوا عَنِ السَّيِّئَاتِ

as-sayyiāt	*ᶜani*	*yaᶜfū*	*wa*	*ᶜibādihi*	*ᶜan*
(the) misdeeds	(from)	forgives	and	His worshippers	from

9. *Any one of you who does a misdeed through ignorance*

man ᶜamila minkum sūᵓam bi-jahālatin

مَنْ عَمِلَ مِنْكُمْ سُوٓءًا بِجَهَٰلَةٍ

bi-jahāḷatin	*sūᵓan*	*minkum*	*ᶜamila*	*man*
in ignorance	a misdeed	from you	did	he who

then repents thereafter and makes amends,

thumma tāba mim baʿdihi wa

ثُمَّ تَابَ مِنْۢ بَعْدِهٖ وَ

wa	*baʿdihi*	*min*	*tāba*	*thumma*
and	after it	(from)	repented	then

then verily He is Forgiving, Merciful (6:54).

aṣlaḥa fa-innahu ghafūrur-raḥīm

أَصْلَحَ فَأَنَّهُ غَفُورٌ رَّحِيمٌ

raḥīm	*ghafūrur*	*fa-innahu*	*aṣlaḥa*
merciful	most-forgiving	then truly He (is)	made amends

10. Whoso does evil or oppresses

may-yaʿmal sūʾan aw yaẕlim

مَنْ يَّعْمَلْ سُوٓءًا أَوْ يَظْلِمْ

yaẕlim	*aw*	*sūʾan*	*yaʿmal*	*man*
oppresses	or	evil	does	he who

his own self and thereafter seeks God's forgiveness

nafsahu thumma yastaghfiri-llāha

نَفْسَهُ ثُمَّ يَسْتَغْفِرِ اللّٰهَ

Allāha	*yastaghfir*	*thumma*	*nafsahu*
God	seeks forgiveness (from)	then	his soul

shall find God most Forgiving, Merciful (4:110).

yajidil-lāha ghāfūrar-raḥīm

يَجِدِ اللّٰهَ غَفُورًا رَّحِيمًا

raḥīm	*ghāfūr*	*Allāha*	*yajid*
merciful	most-forgiving	God	he shall find

11. Those who commit evil

wal-ladhīna ʿamilūs-sayyiʾāt thumma

وَالَّذِينَ عَمِلُوا السَّيِّئَاتِ ثُمَّ

thumma	*as-sayyiʾāt*	*ʿamilū*	*al-ladhīna*	*wa*
then	(the) misdeeds	did	those who	and

then repent thereafter and believe,

tābū mim baʿdihā wa āmanū

تَابُوا مِنْ بَعْدِهَا وَآمَنُوا

āmanū	*wa*	*baʿdihā*	*min*	*tābū*
believed	and	after it	(from)	repented

certainly our Lord is Forgiving, Merciful (7:153).

inna rabbaka mim baʿdihā laghafūrur-raḥīm

إِنَّ رَبَّكَ مِنْ بَعْدِهَا لَغَفُورٌ رَّحِيمٌ

raḥīm	*la-ghafūr*	*baʿdihā*	*min*	*rabbaka*	*inna*
merciful	(is) indeed most-forgiving	after it	(from)	your Lord	truly

12. Those who do not repent are the ones who are wicked (49:11).

mal-lam yatub fa-ūlāʾika humu-ẓ-ẓālimūn

مَن لَّمْ يَتُبْ فَأُولَٰٓئِكَ هُمُ الظَّٰلِمُونَ

az-ẓālimūn	*hum*	*fa-ūlāʾika*	*yatub*	*lam*	*man*
the oppressors	they (are)	then those	repent	did not	he who

Let's find out what you have learned from

Section 3: Self-development:
Fill in the blanks:

1. Turn to God.
2. And seek God's forgiveness!
3. Explain why 9:3 tells us it is better for us to repent.

Section 4: Conclusion

The Quran is a guidance to us. It teaches us not to despair when we find ourselves in difficult situations. Remember we learned "make a decision and then trust in God?" Not getting depressed requires a decision on our part and the decision to reform our life and develop our inner self. We begin to do this by turning to God in repentance for our wrongdoings and asking for His forgiveness.

Section Answers:

Section 2: Dispel Despair and Depression

1. You shall triumph if you are believers.
2. ...his Lord fears not loss or oppression.
3. there is ease.

Section 3: Self-development

1. (66:8).
2. (2:199).
3. Each response differs.

7 Conclusion

Section 1: Introduction

Involving God in all efforts adds beauty and blessings to human labor. The moment we think of God Almighty as a benevolent Friend and as an unfailing Guide, we begin to feel different. We feel the warmth of a new hope, a new purpose and a new confidence. We cease to be weak and lonely. That precisely is the role of the Muslim prescribed prayer. It is a source of powerful motivation to wise and persistent striving. It has been found to possess marvellous potential for putting people on the path to peace and progress.

A sincere prayer, coupled, of course, with right action, never fails. The present chapter presents a selection of thirteen simple prayers from the Holy Quran. They relate to certain major aspects of children's' lives. Worded so beautifully, these prayers find their way into the heart so smoothly. Any child anywhere in the world could avail of their magic impact in any sector of his or her everyday life. Recite just one prayer or any number of them any time you feel like it. It will do you a lot of good. Even if you cannot read the original Arabic words, know that God Almighty understands all languages. Just recite the English version alone. That would do until you are able to pick of Arabic bit by bit.

The prayers of peace and progress are presented here under the following headings:

Section 2: Make me a Good Citizen
Section 3: Forgive My Parents
Section 4: Increase My Knowledge
Section 5: Give Me Wisdom and Good Company
Section 6: Save Me from Ignorance
Section 7: Grant Me Mercy and Success
Section 8: Prevent Me from Going Astray
Section 9: Forgive My Errors and Excesses
Section 10: Bless Me with Patience
Section 11: Lessen My Burdens
Section 12: Protect Me From the Agony
Section 13: May I Be a Muslim Forever
Section 14: Accept My Prayer

Section 2: Make Me a Good Citizen

Our Lord! Give us good in this world

rabbanā ātinā fid-dunyā ḥasanataw-wa

رَبَّنَآ ءَاتِنَا فِي ٱلدُّنۡيَا حَسَنَةً وَّ

wa	*ḥasanatan*	*ad-dunyā*	*fi*	*ātinā*	*rabbanā*
and	good	the world	in	give us	our Lord

and good in the hereafter and protect us

fil-ākhirati ḥasanatuw-wa-qinā

فِي ٱلۡأٓخِرَةِ حَسَنَةً وَّقِنَا

qinā	*wa*	*ḥasanatan*	*al-ākhirati*	*fi*
protect us from	and	good	the hereafter	in

from the torment of the fire (hell) (2:201).

ᶜadhāban-nār

عَذَابَ ٱلنَّارِ

an-nār	*ᶜadhāb*
the Fire	(the) torment (of)

Section 3: Forgive My Parents

Our Lord! Forgive me, my parents,

rabbanā-ghfir lī wa li-wālidayyā

رَبَّنَا اغْفِرْ لِي وَلِوَٰلِدَيَّ

li-wālidayyā	*wa*	*lī*	*ighfir*	*rabbanā*
(to) my parents	and	(to) me	forgive	our Lord

and the believers on the Day of Reckoning (14:41).

wa lil-muᵓminīn yawma yaqumul-ḥisab

وَلِلْمُؤْمِنِينَ يَوْمَ يَقُومُ الْحِسَابُ

al-ḥisab	*yaqumu*	*yawma*	*lil-muᵓminīn*	*wa*
the Accounting	will be established	on the day	(to) the believers	and

Section 4: Increase My Knowledge

My Lord! grant me an increase in knowledge (20:114).

rabbi zidnī ᶜilman

رَّبِّ زِدْنِي عِلْمًا

ᶜilman	*zidnī*	*rabbi*
in knowledge	increase me	My Lord

Section 5: Give Me Wisdom and Good Company

My Lord! Grant me wisdom and

rabbi hab lī ḥukmaw-wa

رَبِّ هَبْ لِي حُكْمًا وَّ

wa	*ḥukman*	*lī*	*hab*	*rabbi*
and	wisdom	to me	grant	my Lord

join me with the righteous (26:83).

alḥiqnī biṣ-ṣāliḥīn

أَلْحِقْنِي بِالصَّٰلِحِينَ

biṣ-ṣāliḥīn	*alḥiqnī*
with the righteous	join me

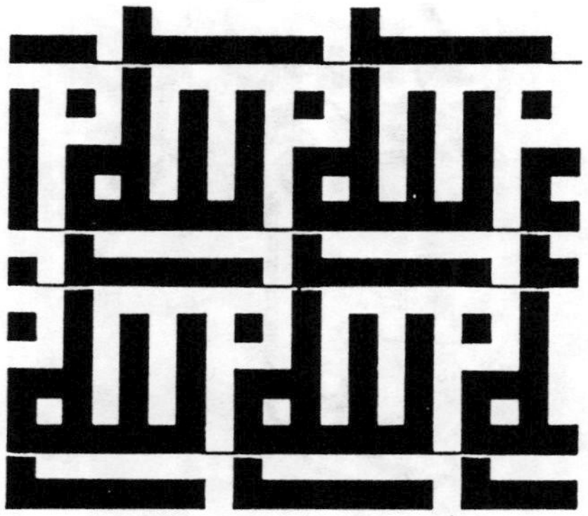

Section 6: Save Me From Ignorance

I seek God's refuge from the ignorant (2:67).

a^{c}ūdhu billāhi an akūna mina-l-jāhilīn

أَعُوذُ بِاللهِ أَنْ أَكُونَ مِنَ الْجٰهِلِينَ

al-jāhilīn	*min*	*akūna*	*an*	*billāhi*	*a^{c}ūdhu*
the ignorant	of	I be	lest	with God	I seek refuge

Section 7: Grant Me Mercy and Success

Our Lord! Give us mercy from Thy presence

rabbanā ātinā mil-ladunka raḥmataw

رَبَّنَآ ءَاتِنَا مِن لَّدُنكَ رَحْمَةً

raḥmatan	*ladunka*	*min*	*ātinā*	*rabbanā*
mercy	Thy presence	from	give us	our Lord

and dispose of our concern in the right way (18:10).

wa hayyīʾu lanā min amirnā rashadan

وَهَيِّئْ لَنَا مِنْ أَمْرِنَا رَشَدًا

rashadan	*amirnā*	*min*	*lanā*	*hayyīʾu*	*wa*
in integrity	our concern	of	for us	dispose	and

Section 8: Prevent Me From Going Astray

Our Lord! Turn not aside our hearts

rabbanā lā tuzigh qulūbanā

رَبَّنَا لَا تُزِغْ قُلُوبَنَا

qulūbanā	*tuzigh*	*lā*	*rabbanā*
our hearts	turn aside	not	our Lord

after Thou hast guided us.

ba^{c}da idh hadaytanā

بَعْدَ إِذْ هَدَيْتَنَا

hadaytanā	*idhba^{c}da*
Thou hast guided us	after

Grant us Thy Mercy for truly

wa hab lanā mil-ladunka raḥmatan innaka

وَهَبْ لَنَا مِن لَّدُنكَ رَحْمَةً

innaka	*raḥmatan*	*ladunka*	*min*	*lanā*	*hab*	*wa*
truly Thou	mercy	Thy presence	from	to us	grant	and

Thou art the Granter (3:8).

anta-l-wahhāb

إِنَّكَ أَنتَ الْوَهَّابُ

al-wahhāb	*anta*
the Granter	Thou (art)

Section 9: Forgive My Errors and Excesses

Our Lord! Forgive us our sins

rabbanā-ghfir lanā dhunūbanā wa

رَبَّنَا اغْفِرْ لَنَا ذُنُوبَنَا وَ

wa	*dhunūban*	*lanā*	*ighfir*	*rabbanā*
and	our sins	(to) us	forgive	our Lord

and wastefulness in our affairs. Make firm

isrāfanā fī amrinā wa thabbit

إِسْرَافَنَا فِيٓ أَمْرِنَا وَثَبِّتْ

thabbit	*wa*	*amrinā*	*fī*	*isrāfanā*
make firm	and	our affair	in	our wastefulness

our feet and help us against the unbelievers (3:147).

aqdāmanā wa-nṣurnā ᶜalā-l-qawmil-kāfirīn

أَقْدَامَنَا وَانْصُرْنَا عَلَى الْقَوْمِ الْكٰفِرِينَ

al-kāfirīn	*al-qawni*	*ᶜalā*	*unṣurnā*	*wa*	*aqdāmanā*
(the) unbelievers	the people	against	help us	and	our feet

Section 10: Bless Me With Patience

Our Lord! Pour forth on us patience.

rabbanā-afrigh ᶜalaynā ṣabraw-wa

رَبَّنَآ أَفْرِغْ عَلَيْنَا صَبْرًا وَّ

wa	ṣabran	ᶜalaynā	afrigh	rabbanā
and	patience	over us	pour out	our Lord

Set firm our feet and help us

thabbit aqdāmanā wa-nṣurnā

ثَبِّتْ أَقْدَامَنَا وَانْصُرْنَا

unṣurnā	wa	aqdāmanā	thabbit
help us	and	our feet	make firm

against the unbelievers (2:250).

ᶜalāl-qawmil-kāfirin

عَلَى الْقَوْمِ الْكٰفِرِيْنَ

al-kāfirin	al-qawmi	ᶜalā
(the) unbelievers	the people	against

Section 11: Lessen My Burdens

Our Lord! Blame us not if we forget.

rabbanā lā tuʾākhidhnā in-nasīnā

رَبَّنَا لَا تُؤَاخِذْنَآ إِن نَّسِينَآ

nasīnā	*in*	*tuʾākhidhnā*	*lā*	*rabbanā*
we forget	if	blame us	not	our Lord

Our Lord! Burden us not with a burden

aw akhṭāʾnā rabbanā wa lā taḥmil ʿalaynā iṣran

أَوْ أَخْطَأْنَا ۚ رَبَّنَا وَلَا تَحْمِلْ عَلَيْنَآ إِصْرًا

iṣran	*ʿalaynā*	*taḥmil*	*lā*	*wa*	*rabbanā*	*akhṭāʾna*	*aw*
a burden	on us	lay	not	(and)	Our Lord	we erred	or

which you placed on our predecessors!

kamā ḥamaltahu ʿalāl-ladhīna min qablinā

كَمَا حَمَلْتَهُۥ عَلَى ٱلَّذِينَ مِن قَبْلِنَا

qablinā	*min*	*āl-ladhīna*	*ʿalā*	*ḥamaltahu*	*kamā*
before us	from	those who (were)	upon	Thou didst lay	like that

Our Lord! Impose not on us

rabbanā wa lā tuḥammilnā mā

رَبَّنَا وَلَا تُحَمِّلْنَا مَا

mā	*tuḥammilnā*	*wa*	*lā*	*rabbanā*
that which	burden us with	and	not	Our Lord!

that for which we have no strength and pardon us and

lā ṭaqata lanā bihi wa-ʿfu ʿannā wa-

لَا طَاقَةَ لَنَا بِهِۦ ۖ وَٱعْفُ عَنَّا وَ

lā	*ṭaqatalanā*	*bihi*	*wa*	*wa-*	*ʿfu*	*ʿannā*	*wa*
(there) is not	power	for us	with it	and	pardon	us	and

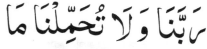

forgive us and have mercy on us.

-ghfir lanā wa-rḥamnā

اغْفِرْ لَنَا وَارْحَمْنَا

irḥamnā	*wa*	*lanā*	*ighfir*
have mercy on us	and	(to) us	forgive

Thou art our Protector, so help us

anta mawlānā fa-nṣurnā

أَنْتَ مَوْلَٰنَا فَانْصُرْنَا

fa-nṣurnā	*mawlānā*	*anta*
so help us	our Protector	Thou (art)

against the unbelievers (2:286).

ᶜalāl-qawmil-kāfirīn

عَلَى الْقَوْمِ الْكَٰفِرِينَ

al-kāfirīn	*al-qawmi*	*ᶜalā*
(the) unbelievers	the people	against

Section 12: Protect Me From the Agony!

Our Lord! We have indeed believed. Forgive

rabbanā innamā āmannā fa-ghfir lanā

رَبَّنَآ إِنَّنَآ ءَامَنَّا فَاغْفِرْ لَنَا

lanā	*fa-ghfir*	*āmannā*	*innamā*	*rabbanā*
(to) us	so forgive	we have believed	truly	our Lord

our sins and save us from the torment of the fire (3:16).

dhunūbanā wa qinā ᶜadhāban-nār

ذُنُوبَنَا وَقِنَا عَذَابَ النَّارِ

an-nār	*ᶜadhāb*	*qinā*	*wa*	*dhunūbanā*
the fire	(the) torment (of)	save us from	and	our sins

Section 13: May I Be a Muslim Forever

Our Lord! Pour out on us patience

rabbanā afrigh ᶜalaynā ṣabraw-wa

رَبَّنَآ أَفۡرِغۡ عَلَيۡنَا صَبۡرٗا وَّ

wa	*ṣabran*	*ᶜalaynā*	*afrigh*	*rabbanā*
and	patience	on us	pour our	our Lord

and cause us to die as Muslims (7:126).

tawaffanā muslimīn

تَوَفَّنَا مُسۡلِمِينَ

muslimīn	*tawaffanā*
as Muslims	make us die

وهو على كل شي قدير

Section 14: Accept My Prayer

Our Lord! Accept (this prayer) from us. Truly Thou art

rabbanā taqabbal minnāinnaka anta-

رَبَّنَا تَقَبَّلْ مِنَّاۖ إِنَّكَ أَنتَ

anta	*innaka*	*minnā*	*taqabbal*	*rabbanā*
Thou (art)	truly Thou	from us	accept	our Lord

the All-hearing, the All-knowing (2:127).

-s-samīcul-calīm

السَّمِيعُ الْعَلِيمُ

al-calīm	*as-samīcu*
the Knower	the Hearer